Splendor at Court

RENAISSANCE SPECTACLE AND THE THEATER OF POWER

Roy Strong

HOUGHTON MIFFLIN COMPANY BOSTON

1973

Printed in Great Britain

Contents

For Julia

Preface

The purpose of this book is a very simple one. It aims to gather together, for the first time, all that has been written since the last war on Renaissance court fêtes. At present no general work exists to introduce the reader to this complex, diffuse, and at the same time profoundly fascinating subject, one which borders on virtually every aspect of Renaissance and Baroque civilization. It has posed many problems in the presentation of material, but in the main festival studies fall broadly into two groups, the theoretical and the pratical, that is, examination of the component parts and the philosophy of the fêtes, as against studies of individual people who were prime exponents of the art. An approach through either one of these aspects was found not to give an entirely satisfactory or complete picture of the role of the fête in sixteenth- and seventeenth-century society. This accounts for the long chapter 'The Politics of Spectacle' preceding studies of festivals associated with particular rulers.

I make no apology for drawing heavily on the work of others who have written in detail about various areas dealt with in shortened form in this book. My debt to them is incalculable. Nor would I have been able to write it without the years of training I received at the Warburg Institute under Frances A. Yates, whose studies of French and English festivals remain classics in the field. The Library and the Photographic Collection have patiently borne the tribulations of my periodic incursions. In the former, I wish to acknowledge with warm gratitude J. B. Trapp, who read the book in typescript and made some extremely pertinent suggestions; in the latter, Elizabeth McCrath, who cheerfully coped with my excavations in the photographic files.

This book is based on the Ferens Lectures in Fine Art for 1971–2, delivered at the University of Hull and subsequently redelivered at the University of Yale, under the auspices of the Mellon Center for British Studies, and at the Victoria and Albert Museum. My first duty is therefore gratefully to acknowledge the permission of the University of Hull authorities to print them in their present form.

The writing of any book owes much to many people and I apologize to anyone whom I have omitted to thank. I acknowledge a significant debt to Stephen Orgel, for it was written at the same time as our joint book *Inigo Jones: The Theatre of the Stuart Court*. The chapter on the Caroline court masque indeed is directly based on conclusions we reached jointly in that book and our frequent conversations on the topic of art and power during the Renaissance stimulated other parts of *Splendour at Court*. Others in particular who helped are Sylvia England, who garnered from the British Museum Library vast piles of xeroxes of festival books, Antonia Fraser and Richard Barber who read the typescript and offered valuable criticism on presentation, Alan Argent for crucial checking, Jane Dorner who gathered the illustrations and Martha Bates, Margaret Willes and Jean Richardson who saw the book through the press. And last but not least my wife, who loyally sat at my feet and listened to me read each chapter as I finished it.

ROY STRONG
October 1973

9

1 Prologue: Fêtes Royales

10 February 1640 was the birthday of Madame Royale, the Duchess Christina of Savoy, sister of Louis XIII and widow of the Duke Victor Amadeus I. That year it was celebrated at the castle of Chambéry by a ballet entitled *Hercules and Love*, invented by her counsellor and devoted friend, Count Filippo Aglié. There is a marvellous pictorial record of this princely spectacle, as indeed of all Savoy fêtes for over twenty years, preserved in a series of volumes written and illuminated by one Tommaso Borgonio. In the ballet Duchess Christina saw her own son, the little Duke Charles Emmanuel, play the part of Love attired in a wonderful costume of cloth of gold and silver, with diminutive wings sprouting from his shoulders, an absurd bunch of multi-coloured ostrich plumes on his head, and clutching a tiny bow and arrow. Not only did she have the delight of seeing her son dance for her, but her eleven-year-old daughter arrived later in the ballet in a ship, along with other court ladies dressed as Cypriots, having voyaged from that island, the haven of Love, to pay tribute to the Duchess and offer her greetings on her birthday. The setting was of rocks backed by a distant seascape and port, on to which sailed a ship with flags fluttering in the wind and on the poop of which perched Cupid aiming his arrow.

By 1640 spectacles of this sort were part of the repertory of entertainment at every court all over Europe. The thirteen volumes of text and illuminations of Savoy court fêtes give a wonderful glimpse into this lost world at its apogee. Before our eyes unfold ballets, tournaments and courtly banquets to celebrate birthdays, marriages, saints' days and carnival time. Knights in exotic costume vanquish sea monsters in the Piazza

1

2

3

Plate IV

OPPOSITE 1 Artist unknown, *Christina, Duchess of Savoy and her Children*

2 *Duke Charles Emmanuel as Love in the Ballet 'Hercules and Love', 1640*

3 *The arrival of Christina's daughter, Adelaide, and other court ladies disguised as Cypriots in the Ballet 'Hercules and Love', 1640*

Plate I   Castello to mark the marriage of Christina's daughter, Adelaide, to
Ferdinand of Bavaria; Madame's own birthday is celebrated by a patriotic
Plate II   banquet followed by a ballet, a feast in which each course took place in a
different room decorated to evoke the provinces of Savoy; or, at an earlier
4   date, she and her husband had boarded the Ship of Felicity in the midst of
the *salle des fêtes* to the roar of cannons, to watch a marine entertainment.
Looking through the drawings, engravings and illuminations of these
endless festivities, we enter a world of fantastic allegory, for these fêtes
were not only for enjoyment but were meant to be read, in the words of
Menestrier, the seventeenth-century theorizer of the court fête, as '*Allegories de l'Estat des temps*'. They are crammed with contemporary com-
ment, but said in a language that is today virtually incomprehensible as a
means of presenting a programme of political ideas.

   Christina's devoted minister and servant Count Filippo Aglié occupied
a key role at the Savoy court, devising these spectacles for a period of over
thirty years. Menestrier himself describes Aglié as a man 'versed in the

knowledge of history, antiquity, politics, and every sort of *belles lettres*, [he] could compose excellent Latin, Italian and French verse, could play all sorts of instruments and compose music'. Year after year Aglié presided over these entertainments, devising the themes, writing the verses, composing the music, supervising the vast team of designers, artists, sculptors, actors and singers which made up each spectacle. He himself was celebrated throughout the Europe of his day as a brilliant choreographer. Aglié's qualifications fitted him for the role exactly, for he possessed a wide literary and artistic knowledge aligned to a detailed grasp of contemporary politics as one of the ducal counsellors of state. Who better could devise '*Allegories de l'Estat des temps*'? Even though his ballet of *Hercules and Love* lives on for us today as little more than a delightful archaic spectacle, a remote ancestor of the creations of Diaghilev, charming with its flat painted side wings and backcloth, its richly attired aristocratic performers, its touches of humanity in the appearance of the Duchess's own children, the ballet was devised and understood by the

4 *Fête for Duchess Christina's Birthday, Turin, 1628*

5 Andrea Vincentino, *The arrival of Henry III in Venice, 1574*

audience at the time as having a quite specifically political connotation.

It is some measure of how far we have lost this way of thinking about court entertainments that this is the last aspect that would cross our minds when examining these glittering performances today. In her birthday ballet of 1640, Madame Royale saw danced before her the hopes and fears of the moment. To grasp a fraction of its impact at the time we have to reconnoitre back in time. Christina's husband, Victor Amadeus I, had unfortunately died in 1637, leaving a young child as his heir. His two brothers, disputing Christina's claim to the regency, had promptly allied themselves with Spain, and two years later Spanish forces actually invaded Piedmont and besieged Turin. Christina fled to France and at Grenoble entered into humiliating transactions with her brother, Louis XIII, and his minister, Cardinal Richelieu. It was Filippo Aglié who saved the Duchess from virtual surrender to France, a surrender which included her infant son being handed over to be educated at the French court. Aglié's ballet *Hercules and Love* celebrated the return of Madame Royale to her exiled court and her reunion with her beloved children. The ballet danced by her son, the infant Duke, and her daughter, together with many of the greatest nobles of the Savoy court, was a reaffirmation of loyalty at a crucial moment in the country's history. The plot, invented by Aglié, told how the Duchess's subjects, the 'Alpine heroes', had been seduced from their allegiance by two wicked enchantresses, Urganda and Melissa (Spain and France), and how this disturbance would alone be quelled and reduced to calm by the Alpine Hercules (the deceased Duke Victor Amadeus) sending Love (the little Duke Charles Emmanuel) to restore concord to her divided peoples. In 1640 this romantic dramatization was a perfectly normal means of expressing a brutal political reality.

By the middle of the seventeenth century such expressions in the language of court spectacle were a natural part of the apparatus of the Baroque monarch. But this concept was initially a creation of the Renaissance mind. To a great extent the court fête and its context represented one of the most profound philosophical positions taken up by Renaissance writers and artists, who genuinely believed in the importance of the role of art and letters in the service of the State. All over Europe poets, architects, painters, sculptors and musicians united to create these ephemeral spectacles. In Venice, in 1574, Tintoretto and Veronese collaborated to decorate an arch designed by Palladio for the entry of Henry III en route from Poland to France; in England, in 1533, Holbein

5

6 Hans Holbein,
Design for a pageant arch of the Muses for the coronation entry of Anne Boleyn into London, 1533

6

designed a pageant of the Muses for the coronation entry of Anne Boleyn into London; earlier, Leonardo da Vinci had devised both Louis XII's entry into Milan and Francis I's into Pavia; Inigo Jones was to expend forty years of his life in supervising the court entertainments of the Stuart kings; and the entry of the Archduke Ferdinand into Antwerp in 1635 was

Plate III made under the artistic direction of Peter Paul Rubens. Writers involved range from Ben Jonson and Thomas Carew to Pierre Ronsard and Jean Dorat; and musicians from Orlando di Lasso to Claudin Le Jeune, and from John Dowland to Claudio Monteverdi. Even the philosopher Descartes devised a ballet for his mistress, Christina, Queen of Sweden. No other art form demonstrates so fully the passionate belief held during the Renaissance of the union of the arts. The court fête could express philosophy, politics and morals through a unique fusion of music, painting, poetry and the dance, all terrestrial manifestations of that overall cosmic harmony which they believed governed the universe and which the art of festival tried so passionately to re-create on earth. Few things, therefore, can give us such a vivid insight into the workings of the Renaissance mind.

2 The Politics of Spectacle

Court festivals focused on the prince. In a Europe dominated by the problem of rival religious creeds and the breakdown of the Universal Church, the monarch not only established himself as the arbiter in religious matters but gradually became adulated as the sole guarantor of peace and order within the State. Before the invention of the mechanical mass media of today, the creation of monarchs as an 'image' to draw people's allegiance was the task of humanists, poets, writers and artists. During the sixteenth and seventeenth centuries the most profound alliance therefore occurred between the new art forms of the Renaissance and the concept of the prince. This proliferated into every field of artistic endeavour. These were the centuries of palace building: the Louvre and Fontainebleau by the Valois, Whitehall and Nonsuch by the Tudors, and the Escorial by the Habsburgs. Simultaneously the State portrait, together with its multiplication by studio assistants and engravers, became a vehicle for dynastic glorification. This was reflected in many miraculous alliances between ruler and painter: Charles V and Titian, Holbein and Henry VIII or Van Dyck and Charles I. Such a systematic proliferation of monarchical imagery equally found expression in the cult of the medal. Every great event in the life of a prince was to be enhanced by recondite allegory on the reverses of medals struck in his honour. Not only did such attitudes affect the visual arts but they also affected the world of letters. The great Renaissance epics, Ronsard's *Franciade* or Spenser's *The Faerie Queene*, were written for the glory of princes. Each celebrated the reigning dynasty by perceiving its members through the mythical history of their legendary forbears. At the same time court historians, under the impact of Renaissance historiography, recast national history within dynastic terms. For Edward Hall the whole of English history was but a prologue to the accession of the house of Tudor and, in particular, to the most magnificent reign of King Henry VIII. For a chronicler of the arts like Vasari the development of painting to perfection was somehow aligned to the rise of the Medici to absolute power within the city of Florence.

To architecture, painting and sculpture, literature and history, one must add the most ephemeral and immediate art form of all, that of festival. The importance attached to tournaments, ballets, state entries, firework displays, water spectacles, alfresco fêtes, intermezzi, masques and masquerades is reflected in the vast corpus of literature printed to commemorate these events. These describe to us, in minute detail, what might, at first glance, seem essentially trivia, the architecture, paintings and decorations,

the sculptures, allegorical devices, scenery and costumes that made up such occasions. These descriptions and their commentaries were to enable those who were not there to savour the transitory wonder and to grasp its import from afar. Commemorative books, with their elaborate illustrations printed under official auspices, were designed to pass to posterity as monuments of princely magnificence.

Why in fact was there what can only be described as a vast explosion of court entertainment throughout Europe for two centuries? How did festivals develop and in what way were they different from their medieval predecessors? Why was there such a profound belief in the power and efficacy of such spectacles which seem to us now totally incomprehensible? As I hope to show, the court fête was the product of various influences and pressures. There were those from below, from the creators, who saw in them not only virtuous employment in the service of the State, but the chance to revive the lost festival forms of classical antiquity. This search for ancient forms led to the revival of the antique *naumachia* or water festival, to the development of State entries as lineal descendants of antique triumphs, to the introduction of the horse ballet in emulation of the ancient Greeks, to the archaeological pursuit of the classical theatre and speculation as to its Vitruvian machinery, which led to the invention of the proscenium arch and perspective stage scenery and, finally, to the humanistic preoccupation with the reconstruction of ancient music and dancing, which resulted in the forbears of our modern opera and ballet. The study of festivals takes us into all these fields and as a result what was once a coherent single artistic statement has, in the hands of modern scholarship, become fragmented. But the thread by which we can retain the coherence they had at the time is the prince. At his behest such 'toys', as Francis Bacon once referred to them, were performed. They celebrated his entry into this world and his departure from it. They marked the great events of both his private and his public life, his marriage, the birth of his children, his victories and treaties of alliance, his coronation and accession day. Through them the prince was able to manifest himself at his most magnificent in the sight of his subjects. By means of myth and allegory, sign and symbol, gesture and movement, festival found a means to exalt the glory of the wearer of the Crown. In such a way the truths of sacred monarchy could be propagated to the court and a tamed nobility take its place in the round of ritual.

The medieval heritage of festival was basically ecclesiastical, celebrating

*Charles V as Count of Flanders
enters Bruges, 1515 (8–13):
8 Artaxerxes promises to restore
Jerusalem: Charles topples
Fortune from her wheel*

the prince in relation to Holy Church, his sacred anointing at his coronation, his presentation of myrrh, frankincense and gold at Epiphany or the
washing of the feet of the poor on Maundy Thursday. These occasions
were inherited by the great dynasties of Europe in the sixteenth century
but extended and overlaid by what might be described as a liturgy of
State. This can be followed in its most extreme form in Protestant
countries, where the splendours of Catholic liturgical spectacle were
banished at the Reformation along with the old medieval saints' days. To
replace these came State-promoted festivals. In England the court and the
people now celebrated instead the ruler's accession and birthday, or days
commemorating deliverance from the hands of Catholic assassins. The
fifth of November, the day of the Gunpowder Plot, was deliberately
elevated to the rank of a State festival by Act of Parliament to recall to
everyone's mind for ever the miraculous escape of James I and his family
from the wicked papists. In Catholic countries the new ecstatic and mystical piety of the Counter-Reformation could be diverted to meditations on
the mystery of the Crown. The creation by Henry III of France of the
Order of the Holy Spirit aimed to draw such pietistic attitudes to the
Valois monarchy. In more violent form, the ceremonial of *auto da fé*
glorified the Spanish Crown as the shield of Holy Faith against the perversions of heresy.

But whether Tudor, Habsburg or Valois, all transmuted the traditional

forms of secular entertainment into a vehicle for dynastic apotheosis. In this way each of the main forms of spectacle inherited from the Middle Ages was eventually touched by the hand of the prince. These can be categorized as the royal entry, the exercise of arms and the indoor divertissement. Each of these forms interconnect yet are separate, each underwent a significant evolution under the impact of Renaissance humanism through the fifteenth and into the sixteenth centuries. An understanding of the fabric of these forms is essential for anyone wishing to read the language of festival. They are vanished means of courtly and popular expression which need to be recreated in order to be understood.

Of the three forms of spectacle the royal entry, when a ruler made his solemn entry into and took possession of a city or town, was the most public. A royal entry reflected the achievements of the present and reviewed those of the past while turning an optimistic eye to the future. The form itself was inherited from the Middle Ages where, until the middle of the fourteenth century, it had been a simple procession. Clergy, town officers, bourgeoisie and members of the guilds met the king at the city gate and conducted him into the town. By the close of the fourteenth century this elementary welcome had been elaborated by the introduction of street pageants, organized by the guilds in the main and almost always religious in theme. Everywhere throughout Europe in the fifteenth and

LEFT 9 *Moses delivers the Tables of the Law: Louis of Nevers grants privileges to Bruges*

RIGHT 10 *The Iron Age of Bruges: Nebuchadnezzar dreams of the tree being eaten away by beasts; Bruges faints while a lawyer and burgher try to retain Merchandise and Gain*

23

into the sixteenth century occur the same archways or street theatres with the same compilation of castles, genealogical trees, tabernacles, fountains and gardens, the same groups of allegorical personages, mainly the Virtues, together with biblical and historical *exempla*. The imagery that is unravelled for the glory of princes stems from the world of the *Songe du Vergier* and the *Roman de la Rose*. The pageants themselves looked like medieval paintings and manuscript illuminations come to life. When Anne of Brittany entered Paris in 1486 on her marriage to Charles VIII, she was greeted by a pageant depicting France as *Vouloir* separated by the figure of War from Brittany as *Sure Alliance*. Nearby the four estates of the realm wailed and wept. At the Princess's approach, Peace suddenly descended from a cloud and War was vanquished.

8–13   Medieval typology, the foreshadowing of present by past events, is admirably caught in the entry of Charles V as Count of Flanders, into Bruges in 1515. In one pageant the young Duke assists Merchandise to depose Fortune from her wheel and replace her with Bruges, an event paralleled by Artaxerxes promising to restore Jerusalem. In another, Louis of Nevers granting privileges to the city is compared to Moses

Plate V   delivering the Tables of the Law. In the same year Francis I entered Lyon with just such a mixture of medieval commonplaces: the baptism of Clovis recalled the sanctity of the kings of France; in a lily twenty feet in height stood Francis I flanked by *Grâce de Dieu* and France; the King was

LEFT II *The Silver Age of Bruges: Jacob departs from the land of Canaan; Merchandise and Gain depart from Bruges*

RIGHT 12 *Alexander riding Bucephalus while Philip of Macedon looks on*

13 *Spanish Pageant. Garden with Orpheus*

glimpsed again guiding the ship of France to victory, while everywhere Virtues and abstractions of the feelings of the moment acted out their welcome to the King in a visual repertory of late medieval Gothicism little touched by the new forms of the Renaissance. Medieval pageantry of this type survived until the late sixteenth century on the fringes of Europe in England, Scotland, the Low Countries and provincial France. Elizabeth I's entry into London in 1559 is still within such a tradition. Devised by Richard Mulcaster, it was deliberately Protestant and propagandist in theme and the events of the day included the presentation to the young Queen of the English Bible. In spite of its reformist ethic, the aesthetic remained medieval: Elizabeth's descent was illustrated in a vast rose tree of the houses of York and Lancaster, there was a pageant in the form of Virtues defeating Vices, another celebrated the Queen's devotion to the biblical beatitudes, another showed a withered and a flourishing landscape to typify a good and bad commonwealth and, finally, there was a vision of Elizabeth as Deborah, consulting with her estates for the good of her realm. Although arranged by a promoter of humanist values in education, there is virtually no evidence of the Renaissance classical repertory of imagery.

During the fifteenth century in Italy, however, the entry had been gradually transmuted into an *à l'antique* imperial triumph, the presentation of the prince as a victorious hero. Italian *condottieri* were the first to

14 Francesco Laurana, *Alfonso the Great enters Naples, 1443*

revive the antique triumph. Castruccio Castracane entered Lucca in 1326 as a Roman *imperator* standing in a chariot, prisoners being driven before him through the streets. In 1443 Alfonso the Great declined the wreath of laurel prepared for him to wear during his solemn entry into Naples, although he entered it in true classical style through a breach made in the walls. Laurana in his sculpture over the gateway to the castle in Naples records the occasion with considerable accuracy. Alfonso was enthroned upon a car drawn by four white horses, a canopy of cloth of gold borne over him by twenty nobles. Cavaliers on horseback attended him, together with one chariot bearing the goddess Fortune, a Genius at her feet, while upon a second stood Julius Caesar upon a revolving globe. Lastly came a gigantic tower, within the medieval tradition, bearing the Virtues. Ten years later Duke Borso d'Este entered Reggio in even more elaborate style. At the city gate he was welcomed by St Prospero, the patron saint of the town, who was seen floating on a cloud with angels supporting a *baldacchino* above his head. Below rotated a circle of cherubims, two of which received the sceptre and keys from the saint, which they promptly delivered to the Duke while angels sang his praises. At this point the first of three pageant cars made its appearance. Drawn by hidden horses a car bearing an empty throne appeared, behind which stood Justice attended by a Genius. At the corner of the chariot sat grey-headed law-givers encircled by angels and banners. Justice and Genius addressed the

14

LEFT 15 *The Triumph of Chastity from Petrarch's 'I Trionfi', 1488*

RIGHT 16 *The Triumph of Fame from Petrarch's 'I Trionfi', 1488*

OVERLEAF II *Allegorical Banquet at Rivoli for the Birthday of Duchess Christina of Savoy, 1645*

Duke, after which there followed a ship pageant and finally a car drawn by unicorns bearing Charity clasping a burning torch. Further on along the route Julius Caesar presented the seven Virtues to Borso, and the triumph ended with the Duke reviewing once more the chariots from a golden throne placed before the cathedral, after which three angels flew down from a nearby building to present him with branches of victorious palm.

By the close of the *quattrocento* this transformation into a Roman imperial triumph, caught in nascent form in Borso's entry, was so complete that Caesar Borgia could actually stage the triumph of Caesar in Rome in 1500. When Louis XII entered Cremona seven years later, he was received with

> *... arcs triumphans à modes antiques ...*
> *Enrichez de dictz Rethoriques*
> *Exaltans la gloire du Roy.*★

Leonardo da Vinci's reception of Louis XII into Milan was even more strictly classical. It is recorded as having been done *'selon l'ancienne coustume des Romains'*,† and its climax was a triumphal car on which there was a seat of Victory supported by Fortitude, Prudence and Renown. The procession passed beneath a magnificent triumphal arch decorated with paintings

★ '... triumphal arches in the manner of antiquity ... enriched with spoken rhetoric exalting the glory of the king.'
† '... according to the ancient custom of the Romans....'

17 Obelisk in Francesco Colonna,
'Hypnerotamachia Poliphili', 1499

18 Obelisk in Henry II's Entry into Lyon, 1548

RIGHT 19 Obelisk surmounted by France in
Henry II's Entry into Paris, 1549

20 Triumphal Arch in Francesco
Colonna, 'Hypnerotamachia
Poliphili', 1499

21 *Obelisk with the Labours of Hercules in Henry IV's entry into Rouen, 1596*

depicting Louis XII's victories and surmounted by an equestrian statue of the King.

By the opening phases of the French wars in Italy at the close of the fifteenth century the transformation of the royal entry into an antique triumph was accomplished. This development was fashioned by a number of influences which during the sixteenth century were also to affect the visual form of the royal entry north of the Alps. There was the tradition of the *trionfi*, as evoked by Petrarch in his poem of the same name, where those of Love, Chastity, Death and Fame pass by in processional style, each with its train of people as *exempla* and each accompanied by appropriate symbols. In illustrated editions these are always shown as pageant cars *à l'antique*, and as such they crossed Europe in the sixteenth century. So too did another significant and highly influential publication, the *Hypnerotamachia Poliphili*, an archaeological romance by Francesco Colonna published by Aldus Manutius in 1499. The novel takes the form of a dream which includes altars with classical inscriptions, obelisks bearing Egyptian hieroglyphs, columns, pyramids, triumphal arches, temples, antique religious ceremonies, and *à l'antique* props of all sorts, including a series of triumphal processions. One bearing Europa and the Bull was drawn by six lascivious centaurs, another with Leda and the Swan was pulled by elephants, yet a third bore Vertumnus and Pomona.

He sate in an ancient fashioned carre, drawne by fower horned fawns or satyrs. … Before the carre and the fower drawing satyrs, there marched two faire Nymphs, the one of them bare a trophae with a praepend and table … the other a trophae of certain greene sprigges fastened togither, and among them divers rurall instruments fastened. These passed on thus after the ancient manner with great ceremonies, and much solemnities.

The *Hypnerotamachia Poliphili* was a popular manifestation of the serious achievements of *quattrocento* antiquarian scholarship. At the court of Mantua this reached its most influential visual manifestation in the series of paintings of the *Triumph of Caesar* executed by Andrea Mantegna for Gian Francesco Gonzaga between 1485 and 1492. Through the engravings by Nicolas Hogenberg and Robert Péril, these were similarly to have a European influence on the royal entry. Mantegna used all the resources of early Renaissance antiquarian scholarship. He had studied the arch of Titus, read Appian's description of the triumph of Scipio, followed Suetonius' narrative of the triumph of Caesar, and was probably even

31

ABOVE AND RIGHT 22 and 23 *The Triumph of Leda in Francesco Colonna,*
'Hypnerotamachia Poliphili', 1499

familiar with Flavius Josephus' account of Vespasian's triumph. Into the
background he inserts Trajan's column, the arch of Sergii in Pola and the
pyramid of Cestus. The most important source for him was an antiquarian
publication, Valturio's *De Re Militari*, published in Verona in 1472.
Mantegna's procession consists of less than seventy figures, and yet he pur-
veys the impression of teeming thousands: trumpeters, standard-bearers,
25, 26   youths carrying paintings of vanquished cities, prisoners bowed in chains,
banner- and trophy-bearers, huge urns glittering with treasure, culminating in the figure of Caesar himself seated aloft upon a triumphal chariot.

Through the Italian wars and the dissemination of books and engravings
the impact north of the Alps during the first half of the sixteenth century
was enormous. By the beginning of the 1530s it had begun radically to

24 *The Triumph of Vertumnus and Pomona in Francesco Colonna,
'Hypnerotamachia Poliphili', 1499*

Plate VI   transform the French royal entry, so much so that by 1550, when Henry II
entered Rouen, he was presented with a complete re-enactment of a
Roman imperial triumph. Following the surrender of Boulogne by the
English, this entry came at the apogee of his reign. The procession began
27   with a chariot laden with trophies and bearing the figure of Death chained
at the feet of Fame. Next came fifty-seven of the King's Ancestors crowned
28   and wearing splendid robes, figures on horseback who were to act as
exempla to the present monarch. There followed a chariot drawn by uni-
29   corns on which stood Vesta, the goddess of Religion, attended by Royal
Majesty, Virtue Victorious, Reverence and Fear. This alluded to the
King's religious policy of restoring peace and unity, in particular the reunion of the Catholic Church, an aim referred to in the church held aloft

25 Andrea Mantegna, *The Triumph of Caesar: the Elephants*

26 Andrea Mantegna, *The Triumph of Caesar: Chariot bearing Caesar*

Procession on the occasion of Henry II's
Entry into Rouen, 1550 (27–33):
27 *The Triumph of Fame*

28 *The King's Ancestors*

by Vesta. Next marched six bands of military men carrying models of forts won by the King in the area of Boulogne and banners depicting landscapes of the Scottish lowlands won from the English. After these ambled elephants and then figures in chains, alluding to the sad parade of prisoners that had taken place before the beleaguered Boulogne. Flora and her nymphs gaily scattering flowers ushered in the final chariot bearing *'un beau et elegant personnage'*★ representing Henry II, with his four children at his feet, to whom Fortune proferred an imperial diadem. Created under the guidance of local humanists, this entry drew on printed sources on triumphs and was a deliberate attempt to excel a festival form of antiquity. The chariots were *'à l'immitation expréssé des Romains triumphateurs'*† and as a whole the spectacle was *'Pareil triumphe à tous ceulx des Caesars'*.‡

   The royal entry thus became an essential part of the liturgy of secular apotheosis. It was a vehicle whereby public acclamation could be focused on the person of the ruler as the incarnation of the State, the anointed of God, the *pater patriae*, the defender of Holy Church and of Religion, the heir of mighty ancestors, the source of all beneficence whose rule showers peace, plenty and justice on his subjects, and causes the arts to flourish. During the sixteenth century, therefore, the solemn entry became an important part of the cult of the monarch as hero. The word 'triumph' is applied to the royal entry and spreads across Europe in the flood of commemorative literature. Eleanor of Austria's entry into Paris in 1530 is *'triumphante et somptueuse'*, Henry II's into Lyon in 1548 is *'superbe et Triumphante'*, Elizabeth of Valois' into Toledo in 1560 is *'regale et trionfante'*. This change in form included, in general, a shift from *tableaux vivants* and street theatres to classical triumphal arches covered with mute emblems and allegories in paint and sculpture. Even where such rigid

★ 'A handsome and elegant figure.'
† '... deliberate imitations of Roman triumphs'.
‡ '... a triumph equal to those of the Caesars'.

36

29 *The Triumph of Religion*

30 *Soldiers bearing banners*

classicism did not assert itself, as, for example, in England and the Low Countries, a shift in iconography and imagery eventually took place.

Parallel with these developments in the conventions of the royal entry rulers promoted what might be described as a deliberate revival of chivalry. Although the feudal realities of medieval chivalrous society had gone, the patterns of its behaviour and mythology lived on, were indeed, one could say, revitalized in the court life evolved by Tudor, Valois and Habsburg. Chivalric attitudes and values were overlaid by a fashionable Neo-Platonic gloss, traceable, for instance, in handbooks of courtly behaviour, typified above all in Castiglione's *Il Cortegiano*. Romances of chivalry enjoyed an enormous vogue, from the *Armadis de Gaule* to Ariosto's *Orlando Furioso*, from Tasso's *Gerusalemme Liberata* to Spenser's *The Faerie Queene*. In the court fête this is manifested in the continued vitality of the tournament in its three main forms: the tilt, in which knights broke lances against each other across a barrier; the tourney, in which rival parties of knights fought in a *mêlée*; and the barriers, in which

31 *Elephants laden with spoils*   32 *Bound captives*

33 *The King's chariot*

knights exchanged blows on foot across a barrier, a feat of arms often performed indoors rather than alfresco. Although the tournament was still regarded as military training even at the close of the fifteenth century, it had already developed as an artistic form of expression in its own right. As early as the thirteenth century the adoption of fancy dress with increasing elaboration of décor for tournaments became normal, but the stream of development which is significant for Renaissance court fêtes is the one running from the stupendous productions organized by Réné of Anjou and those staged under the auspices of the Dukes of Burgundy. These transformed the tournament into a predetermined romantic saga which was always to find its hero and heroine in the king and his consort.

Plate VII   Réné of Anjou, scholar, poet, artist, architect, courtly lover and valiant knight at arms, maintained a brilliant court. Not only was he the author of the most meticulous treatise on tournament ceremonial ever written, *Le Livre des Tournois*, but he presided over several fantastic feats of arms in which the element of actual combat was made subservient to a carefully rehearsed dramatic plot. The *Pas de la Bergère* at Tarascon in 1449 may be taken as typical of his development of the tournament into a romantic drama. For this event the setting included a thatched cottage occupied by a shepherdess, the lady of the tournament, who tended a fold of sheep, and a tilt where knights, in fancy dress as shepherds, could ride forth from pavilions disguised as cottages.

At the Burgundian court the pattern was elaborated into a mould upon which chivalrous exercises were to be based during the next century and a half. The *Pas de l'Arbre d'Or*, staged in 1468 to celebrate the marriage of Margaret of York to Charles the Bold, is typical of one of many spectacular feats of arms at the Burgundian court. It began with the circularization of a cartel giving the allegorical framework of the tournament. In this the Lady of the *Ile Cellée* begged the Bastard of Burgundy,

RIGHT III Rubens, *Sketch for the Arch of the Mint for the entry of the Cardinal Archduke Ferdinand into Antwerp, 1635*

38

who had recently rescued the lady, to undertake an enterprise, one condition of which was that he should decorate a golden tree with the arms of
famous warriors. The lady placed at the Bastard's disposal her pursuivant,
Arbre d'Or, a dwarf, and the giant of the *Forêt douteuse*, whom she held
captive. The tournament, which took place in the market-place at Bruges,
lasted several days. Opposite the gallery in which the ladies sat there was a
vast golden tree, and each knight arrived with his own separate device

34 *Tournament costume
for Henry VIII, c. 1530*

35 *Carrousel costume for Louis XIV, 1662*

within the overall story of the tilt. The Comte de Roussy, for example, came enclosed within a castle attended by musicians and a dwarf. It was explained that he was held prisoner by a certain lady and could obtain his release only by the intercession of other ladies. Such intercession being granted, the dwarf unlocked the castle gate and the knight rode out in full armour.

This form of romantic dramatization, so highly developed at the courts

anische
mbassa,
dor

Königin
garetha
tz

36 *Carrousel in the Place Royale on the occasion of the announcement of the marriage of Louis XIII to Anne of Austria, 1612*

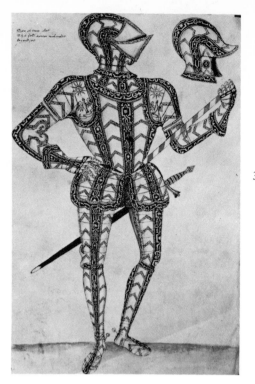

37 *Sir Henry Lee's tournament armour*

of Anjou and Burgundy, usually combined with careful stage-management to ensure that the monarch or heir apparent was always the victor, became the norm for court fêtes. The pattern of these prestige spectacles, in which the myths of medieval romance were deliberately harnessed to the Crown, was followed both by the Emperor Maximilian I and by the young Henry VIII. The legendary Field of Cloth of Gold in 1520 offers the most staggering example of conspicuous consumption to no avail in this sphere, although motivated by a genuine belief that the political problems of Europe would be solved if only monarchs met over a conference table and reduced their wars to chivalrous sports. In the second half of the century the momentum did not decline, although there was a further diminishment in the actual fighting, caused by the death of Henry II at a tournament in 1559. 'Running at tilt is a generous and a Martiall exercise,' wrote Henry Peacham in 1634, 'but hazardous and full of danger, for so many hereby (even in sport) have lost their lives, that I may omit *Henry* the French king, with many other princes and other noble personages of whom History is full.' The result of this was the *joute mascarade* and *carrousel* with its predetermined plot set amidst the most complex of *mises-en-scène*. This became a standard vehicle for expressing princely magnificence, whether, for instance, to celebrate a treaty of alliance in France in 1612 or to mark a great marriage in Savoy in 1650.

34

36
Plate I

44

35 That Louis XIV could still deploy himself as a knight on horseback, the hero of a spectacular tournament in 1662, gives some indication of the vitality of the chivalrous tradition within Europe during the Renaissance and the Baroque periods.

A more specific instance of this deliberate use of chivalry by the Crown is to be found in late sixteenth-century England. The reign of Elizabeth I witnessed one of the most remarkable revivals of chivalry centring on the cult of the Virgin Queen. In a society split by the religious divisions of Catholic, Anglican and Puritan, the ritual of chivalry cut right across the religious barriers. Under the inspiration and guidance of her Master of the Armoury, Sir Henry Lee, the Queen presided over a spectacular series of 37 tournaments held each year on the anniversary of her accession to the throne, 17 November. These were spectacles to which the public, for a small sum, was admitted. Nobles and gentlemen broke their lances in her honour at tilt, arriving in fancy dress, each one weaving a romantic story round his disguise in complement to the Queen. A visiting German gives a vivid if bemused account of the tournament of 1584:

> Many thousand spectators, men, women and girls, got places, not to speak of those who were within the barrier and paid nothing. During the whole time of the tournament all those who wished to fight entered the lists by pairs, the trumpets being blown at the time and other musical instruments. The combatants had their servants clad in different colours, they, however, did not enter the barrier, but arranged themselves on both sides. Some of the servants were disguised like savages, or like Irishmen, with the hair hanging down to the girdle like women, others had horse manes on their heads, some came driving in a carriage, the horses being equipped like elephants, some carriages were drawn by men, others appeared to move by themselves; altogether the carriages were of very odd appearance. ... When a gentleman with his servant approached the barrier ... one of his servants in pompous attire ... addressed the Queen in well-composed verses or with a ludicrous speech, making her and her ladies laugh.

The surviving speeches evoke a picture that is wholly romantic in sentiment. One is spoken by the Damsel of the Queen of Fairies on behalf of an Enchanted Knight, who cannot tilt because 'his armes be locked for a tyme'. There is a sonnet on behalf of a Blind Knight, who has been overcome by the Queen, 'best flower of flowers, that grows both red and white'. Another introduces the Black Knight and his companions, the Wandering Knights, who have been cast into melancholy because they were unable to attend the previous year's tournament (evidence that these

38 Inigo Jones, *Setting for the 'Barriers' of 1610. St George's Portico with Chivalry, right, in a cave*

47

shows unfolded a continuous narrative), but who now return 'to make short payment of the debts of our harts for the honoring of this day'. Evidence suggests that these tilts were serious expressions of the political fabric of the reign. After Sir Philip Sidney's death in 1586 his horse was solemnly led, draped in black, across the tiltyard. Was there, we may wonder, a tearful pause while the Queen and her subjects remembered Philisides, her shepherd knight?

This deliberate use of romantic chivalry to draw knights in allegiance to the Crown stretches into the new reign. Around James I's elder son, Henry, Prince of Wales, there similarly centred a chivalrous revival. Ben Jonson's *Barriers* of 1610 deploys the Prince within a dramatic scenario as the reviver of chivalry. Amid the ruins of the House of Chivalry King Arthur appeared and lowered down from the sky a shield for the Prince, known in his tournament guise as Meliadus. Immediately this was hung up on his tent Lady Chivalry stirred herself within her trophy-hung cave and exclaimed:

> ... O, I could gaze a day
> Upon his armour that hath so revived
> My spirits, and tels me that I am long-lived
> In his appearance. Break, you rusty doors,
> That have so long been shut, and from the shores
> Of all the world come knighthood like a flood ...

Even when exercises of arms of this sort were finally abandoned at the close of James I's reign, the mythology of chivalry was assimilated into that of the court masque.

39 *Henry, Prince of Wales fighting at the Barriers*

The indoor fête was the least developed form of princely magnificence at the opening of the sixteenth century but, by its close, it was well on the way to eclipsing and replacing all other means of celebrating monarchs. The medieval inheritance was one of rudimentary disguisings and mummings, the *entremêts* of the Burgundian court. Huge pageant cars were wheeled into the banqueting hall bearing actors, musicians, singers and maskers in fancy dress. A typical example of this hybrid genre was an entertainment given for the French ambassador by Henry VIII at Greenwich in 1518 to mark the signing of the so-called Treaty of Universal Peace, by which the Princess Mary was to marry the Dauphin and European rulers were to be eternally united in peace against the Infidel. This began with Turks beating drums, after which the horse Pegasus entered with Report as his rider. The horse, oddly enough, was the first spokesman, for, he explained, he had flown across the earth announcing the good news of the impending marriage. After this a curtain was lowered revealing a pageant car with a castle, a rock and a gilded cave, the entrance to which was veiled and behind which sat nine ladies holding wax candles. Musicians were hidden within the rock and nine youths in identical costumes sat upon it. Out of it grew five symbolic trees: an olive tree for the Pope; a fir tree for the Emperor; a lily for the King of France; a rose for Henry VIII; and, finally, a pomegranate, for the King of Spain. A girl dressed as a queen lay stretched between the olive and rose tree bearing a dolphin in her lap. Report explained that the latter signified the marriage, while the rock represented the treaty. At this point a Turk entered challenging the peace, which led into a tourney between fifteen Turkish and fifteen Christian knights. After the latter had presumably triumphed the car moved across the hall to stop before Henry VIII, at which point the most beautiful music was to be heard from the instrumentalists encased within it. It was then wheeled back to its former resting-place and the nine beautiful ladies and attendant youths descended to dance.

Entertainments such as this, with a basis in allegory requiring elucidation in speech, with music, both instrumental and vocal, a simple dramatic plot with a dénouement, often in combat, and, above all, as the climax to the spectacle, choreographed dances by ladies and gentlemen, were common to every European court in the sixteenth century. Out of these disparate ingredients humanists, aided by royal patronage, developed new forms of fêtes: in Florence, the famous intermezzi and subsequently opera; in France, the *ballet de cour*, ancestor of classical ballet; and in England the court masque.

OVERLEAF IV *Carrousel to celebrate the Duke of Savoy's Birthday, 1645*

49

Within these three main forms of entry, tournament and masquerade, Renaissance court fêtes used a common language in glorifying the prince, that is, the language of humanist allegory and symbolism. The growth and promotion by rulers of the court fête through the sixteenth and into the seventeenth century went hand in hand with the spread of humanist classical imagery. History was the Roman history of Livy and Caesar, literature was Virgil, Ovid, Horace, Catullus, the poets of the golden age. The heroes and events they described were applied to the rulers and political situations of the present, ennobling princes and giving contemporary history a grandeur that its reality often lacked. The medieval Church had used allegory to transmit the truths of the faith; humanists now had recourse to the images of antiquity, to the whole resurrected pantheon of the pagan gods, to express abstract ideals of rulership. The imagery of the prince in the fêtes is therefore closely related to developments within the *speculum principis* tradition, those handbooks describing the virtues necessary for princes. A specific example would be *Le Livre de la police humaine* by Gilles d'Avrigny, in which all princely virtues are epitomized by Julius Caesar: the political force of war; the need for a prince to excel in military skill; the importance of reputation; the joys of peace; and the necessity of liberality, especially to men of letters. This, for example, had a considerable influence on the content of Henry II's entry into Rouen in 1550. Renaissance mirrors, like court festivals, endlessly parade the illustrious figures of antiquity as *exempla* of virtues and vices for the ideal ruler. Working under the aura of a pervasive Neo-Platonism, the heroes of antiquity – Augustus, Alexander, Aeneas and a host of others – became 'Ideas' of a particular virtuous or vicious abstraction made flesh. Renaissance mirrors of princes indeed very much resemble court fêtes in that in them too the noble examples and the monstrous tyrants of antiquity parade before the spectators' eyes to illustrate the virtues of princes and the vices of tyrants. By the third decade of the seventeenth century absolutist rulers are not only hymned as embodying the virtues of gods and heroes, they are actually celebrated as surpassing them. In England and France exponents of absolutist principles represent the monarch almost as God. Charles I and Louis XIII are deployed in their festivals as all-handsome, just and powerful, bringers of peace and plenty, as separate from other human beings.

Le Ballet de la Délivrance de Renaud, 1617 (40—5):
40 The Demon Mountain

41 The Enchanted Garden

Sir John Harington in the preface to his translation of Ariosto's *Orlando Furioso* usefully defines the layers of meaning which, under the impact of humanism, would govern a Renaissance court spectacle in the same way as they formed the basis for the composition of a poetic epic. Both were concerned not only with giving delight and pleasure to the ladies but also in purveying matter for contemplation by the learned.

The Ancient Poets have indeed wrapped as it were in their writings divers and sundry meanings, which they call the senses or mysteries thereof. First of all for the literall sense ... they set downe in manner of an historie the acts and notable exploits of some persons worthy memorie: then in the same fiction, as in a second rime and somewhat more fine, as it were nearer to the pith and marrow, they place the Morall sence profitable for the active life of man, approving vertuous actions and condemning the contrarie. Many time also under the self same words they comprehend some true understanding of Naturall Pholosophie, or sometimes of politik governement, and now and then of divinitie: and these same sences that comprehend so excellent knowledge we call the Allegorie, which Plutarch defineth to be when one thing is told, and by that another is understood.

53

42 *Armide and her Monsters*

43 *The Monsters Metamorphosed*

The Renaissance court fête, as it finally evolved during the second half of the sixteenth century into the set forms of entry, *ballet de cour*, intermezzi, court masque and allegorical exercise of arms, was increasingly patterned on these thought assumptions.

Le Ballet de la Délivrance de Renaud danced at the French court in 1617 may be taken as an example of this allegorical method. Based on an episode in Tasso's *Gerusalemme Liberata*, the ballet opened with a mountain in which twelve demons, one of which was played by Louis XIII, kept the knight Renaud prisoner. The demons celebrate their conquest with a dance, after which the location changes to a garden in which a nymph, who arises from a fountain, attempts to seduce two soldiers. Renaud appears and the soldiers, in turn, appeal to him, but he only exults in what he believes to be his god-like existence. This is followed, however, by the knights causing Renaud to look at himself in a crystal shield which they bear. As a result of this Renaud is filled with a revulsion against himself and, moving towards the middle of the room, tears off the jewels, flowers and other

40

41

54

44 *The Hermit and Godefroy's Army*   45 *Godefroy enthroned with his Knights*

ornaments that epitomize his voluptuous enslavement. In the following
scene the enchantress Armide, into whose hands Renaud has fallen, sum-
42 mons up her demons, who appear in the form of monsters. Armide
touches these with her wand and they change again, this time into ridicu-
43 lous old people who execute a grotesque and eccentric dance. On to the
stage next comes a pageant car carrying a wood, behind every tree of
which stands a soldier of the crusader Godefroy's army. These celebrate
44 the escape of Renaud in a dialogue with a hermit:

> *Enfin la raison de retour*
> *Se voit en luy triompher de l'Amour.*
> *Ce tiran n'est plus son vainqueur,*
> *Ses feux ne brûle* [sic] *plus son coeur.*★

45 The ballet comes to its close with a vision of Godefroy enthroned, to-

★ Reason, returning to him, at last emerges victorious over Love. That tyrant is his conqueror no
more, its flame consumes his heart no more.

55

gether with his knights, in a pavilion of cloth of gold, after which they descend to dance the grand ballet.

Louis XIII himself chose the subject of this spectacle. The literal sense is the story from Tasso of Renaud and his deliverance from the enchantress Armide. For the moral sense Renaud represented wayward youth saved through self-realization – the moment when he saw himself in the crystal shield – and through knowledge, in the form of the hermit, sent by Godefroy, the leader of a divinely inspired army, symbolizing intelligence. But the real meaning of the entertainment was political. It was performed during a crucial period in which the government was in the hands of the King's mother, Marie de' Medici, and her favourite Concini, and when the King himself was still under the sway of Luynes. The background to the ballet is the unrest that marked the autumn of 1616, months in which Concini fled from Paris on a wave of unpopularity, in which the King arrested the Prince de Condé and the other princes who had taken up arms, while in the south the Huguenots were restless. All this resulted in a ballet whose central idea was that of a strong king. Louis danced two roles, that of a demon of fire and that of Godefroy. Fire was the most important of the elements, and the ballet elaborated its virtues: *'epurer les corps impurs'*; *'réunir les choses Homogenées et semblables'*;★ it separates gold from silver and achieves that ultimate in royal policy: *'rappeler tous ses sujets a leur devoir, et les purger de tous pretextes de desobeissance.'*† At the close, in the figure of Godefroy, the King appeared as the absolute monarch triumphant over vices and enemies. Shortly after this performance Louis made a *coup d'état* in which the Maréchal d'Ancre was assassinated and his own mother confined to Blois.

The Renaissance court festival stemmed from a philosophy which believed that truth could be apprehended in images. Its approach can be summed up in the words of Prospero conjuring up the marvels of the masque in *The Tempest*: 'No tongue! all eyes! be silent.' Fêtes speak to the visual sense in a lost vocabulary of strange attributes which we can no longer easily read but which, by the close of the sixteenth century, was a perfectly valid silent language within the make-up of the educated Renaissance mind. Our guide to it is another vast tract of literature, books of

★ 'To purify impure hearts'; 'to bring together Homogeneous and similar things.'
† 'Remind all subjects of their duty, and purge them of any excuse for being disobedient.'

Ex bello pax.

En galea,intrepidus quam miles gesserat: & quæ
Sæpius hostili sparsa cruore fuit.
Parta pace apibus tenuis concessit in usum
Alueoli:atque fauos grataque mella gerit.
Arma procul iaceant,fas sit tunc sumere bellum:
Quando aliter pacis non potes arte frui.

Impossibile.

Abluis Aethiopem,quid frustra?ah desine,noctis
Illustrare nigræ nemo potest tenebras.

E 2

ABOVE LEFT 46 'Ex bello Pax' from Alciati, 'Emblemata', 1581
ABOVE RIGHT 47 'Impossibile' from Alciati, 'Emblemata', 1581
LEFT 48 'Pietas Filiorum in Parentes' from Alciati, 'Emblemata',
1581

emblems and *imprese* and mythological manuals.

The passion for emblems began with the *Hieroglyphica*, supposedly written by an ancient Egyptian, Horus Apollo, a manuscript of which was brought to Florence in 1419. At the time it was held to be an ideographical form of writing by which Egyptian priests had recorded sacred mysteries. As sight ranked high in the Neo-Platonic hierarchy, great store was laid on the cult of hieroglyphs and emblems, which, it was believed, not only visually symbolized an abstract idea but somehow by these ancient attributes partook of its very essence. The principles of the *Hieroglyphica* were translated into more popular form by Alciati, whose *Emblemata*, first published in 1531, had run into innumerable editions by the close of the sixteenth century. In this way a swarm of bees making a helmet into a hive symbolized *Pax*, Peace, or two white men scrubbing a coloured one epitomized *Impossibile*, the Impossible, or Aeneas carrying his aged father, Anchises, depicted *Pietas*, Filial Piety. More obscure were the ones stemming back to the *Hieroglyphica*, such as the serpent devouring its own tail representing Time. Compilers of court fêtes eagerly studied these books. Alciati's was already in use for Charles V's entry into Paris in 1540, and by 1560 it was being used in Spain for the entry of Elizabeth of Valois into Toledo.

46, 47
48

This cult of emblems was complemented by a preoccupation with personal devices or *imprese*, a Neo-Platonic revamping of the devices of medieval chivalry. Here, too, there was a vast outpouring of literature, this time continuing throughout the seventeenth century. Layers of abstruse meaning could be extracted from a device such as Henry II's crescent moon and the motto *Donec totum impleat orbem*, which combined prophecies of French imperial expansion and religious aspirations, together with a compliment to his moon-goddess mistress, Diane de Poitiers.

49

All over Europe monarchs deliberately developed complicated personal imagery used in decorating not only their palaces and public buildings but even the most menial items of everyday life – book-bindings, fabrics, silver, glass and dress. The choice by monarchs of personal devices and mottoes could embody powerful political statements. James I's identification of himself with the Old Testament King Solomon by the adoption of the motto *Beati Pacifici* was a statement of his political aspirations as the peacemaker of Europe aligned to his office as a king by Divine Right. In the light of this motto we are able to read the meaning of Ben Jonson's

ENRICO
SECONDO RE DI
FRANCIA

DONEC TOTVM IMPLEAT ORBEM

49 *Moon 'impresa' of Henry II*

courtly masques. Louis XIV so relentlessly identified himself with the Sun that he is still even now thought of as *le Roi Soleil*. In a post-Copernican universe the planets significantly revolved round the Sun, as the choreography of the ballets in which he danced would have made clear in a way more easily understood by the onlooking court.

59

50 *Apollo from Vincenzo Cartari, 'Le Imagini de i dei degli Antichi', 1571 edition*

51 Giorgio Vasari, *Design for the car of Apollo in the mascarade 'La Genealogia degli Dei de'gentili', Florence, 1566*

52 Giorgio Vasari,
*Thought in the mascarade
'La Genealogia degli Dei
de'gentili', Florence, 1566*

These emblem books were complemented by the mythological manuals, which in their turn codified and moralized the stories of classical antiquity and were standard books of reference on the shelves of every educated person. These were Lilio Gregorio Giraldi's *De deis gentium varia et multiplex historia* (1548), Piero Valeriano's *Hieroglyphica sive de sacris Aegyptiorum literis commentarii* (1556), Vincenzo Cartari's *Le imagini de i dei degli Antichi* (1566), Natale Conti's *Mythologiae* (1581) and Cesare Ripa's *Iconologia* (1593). All these ran into many editions, mostly profusely illustrated, and were translated into Italian, German, French and English. Giraldi and Cartari were used, for example, for the *mascherata* of 1566 on the occasion of the marriage of Francesco de'Medici and Joanna of Austria. The *Genealogia degli Dei* had pageant cars by Vasari bearing the strangest of assemblages of deities: the Demogorgon of Boccaccio, the Juno of Martianus Capella or the Assyrian Apollo of Macrobius' *Saturnalia*. For the latter, the compilers of the programme pillaged Cartari.

52

The lengths to which they went to pile up obscure imagery can be captured in the personification of Thought, conceived as an old man. His head-piece consisted of peach stones, the skin of which was serrated by intersecting canals, 'just as the human soul is lacerated by thought' – a symbol drawn from Valeriano's *Hieroglyphica*. Few at the time can have appreciated this pyrotechnic of erudition. All these were derived from the mythological manuals which were likewise the basis for the attributes of the famous intermezzi of 1586 and 1589. Similarly, such manuals were used by Ben Jonson and Inigo Jones in the preparation of the Stuart court masques. *Furor Poetico* is lifted almost unaltered by Inigo Jones from Cesare

53
54

Ripa for the character of Entheus in Thomas Campion's *Lords' Masque* of 1613. There were, of course, bitter complaints from those who could not read the attributes, but Ben Jonson roundly declared that the object of such princely spectacles was to 'declare themselves to the sharpe and learned' and as for the rest, no doubt they 'did gaze, said it was fine and were satisfied'.

FVROR POETICO.

53 *'Furor Poetico' from
Ripa, 'Iconologia', 161*

Henry II's Entry into Lyon, 1548:
LEFT 55 *The Temple of Honour and Virtue*
RIGHT 56 *The Perspective of Troy*

The sixteenth and seventeenth centuries were the age of the allegorical tableau. Festivals are one aspect of this pattern of purveying ideas by a combination of more or less naturalistic pictorial representations on the one hand with, on the other, some kind of organization in space which is not naturalistic but artificial, schematic or diagrammatic. Court fêtes are aggregates of images held together by the printed, spoken or inscribed word which continued to form an integral part of the spectacle, whether a moving or a static one. As the Renaissance court fête evolved into the Baroque, there developed an increasing fascination for presenting diagrams in allegorical tableaux. The latter, therefore, may be said to have occupied for a period a position somewhere between the aural and the visual worlds of communication. As a mode for purveying ideas it was

64

finally to be supplanted by Reason. Shaftesbury in 1713 could quite bluntly dismiss emblem books as 'magical, mystical, monkish, and Gothic'. With this attitude the thought assumptions that had created the Renaissance court fête as a means for communicating ideas and channelling information had vanished.

Developments in form and content were paralleled by transformations in décor. The taste for *à l'antique* architecture could be more instantly realized in the court fête than in any more permanent form. Through festival scenery classical humanist theories concerning harmony and proportion in building were promoted, and some of the wildest extravaganzas of Renaissance architects realized. Lyon was the intellectual capital of France in the

Henry II's Entry into Paris, 1549 (57–61):
57 *The Arch of Gallia*

58 *The Arch of Argo*

first half of the sixteenth century and, because of the large Italian colony in the form of bankers and merchants, it became the key centre for the dissemination of Italian culture. There had been a solitary arch *à l'antique* for Francis I in 1515, but thirty-three years later his son's entry was entirely in the antique manner. The medieval *tableaux vivants* were jettisoned in favour of mute arches bearing allegorical sculpture, paintings, emblems and classical inscriptions, part of a reception which included a view in perspective of classical buildings, a Roman gladiatorial combat and a *naumachia, 'con galere fatto al modo antiquo'*.★ The following year the architect who was responsible for the Lyon entry, Jean Martin, presided over Henry II's entry into Paris. Once more this was an opportunity for

55, 56

57–61

★ '... with ships built in the antique manner'.

67

Martin, the translator of Vitruvius, Serlio and Alberti into French, to make an uncompromising visual statement equal to that made in sculpture by Jean Goujon and that in literary content by the Pléiade. The arches are described as having been built by a second Vitruvius, the proportions of the Corinthian columns are recorded as having been made '... *selon la reigle qu'en baille messire Léon Baptiste Albert, qui faict monstrer l'ouvrage de trop meillure grâce que celle de Vitruve*'.★ The Paris and Lyon entries epitomized an aesthetic revolution.

★ '... according to the rule given by Léone Baptista Alberti, whose buildings are even more graceful than those of Vitruvius'.

59 *The Fountain of Jupiter with the three Fortunes, of the King, of the Nobility and of the People*

In Spain there was a similar progression. Sebastiano Serlio's *Architettura* was translated in 1552, running into two more editions by the close of the century, and Vitruvius was translated in 1582. The earliest recorded use of Vitruvius is in the entry of Elizabeth of Valois into Toledo in February 1560, the incredibly complex arches of which are described as being '*a lo Romano*' or 'as the ancient Greeks made'. In England this architectural statement came even later in the entry of James I into London in March 1604. The arches erected by Stephen Harrison, curiously archaic though they may seem to the modern eye, were manifestations, under the direction of Ben Jonson and Thomas Dekker, of Renaissance classical scholar-

60 *Arch in the form of a letter H for Henry II*

62

LEFT 61 *Arch at the entrance to the Palace*

RIGHT 62 *James I's Entry into London, 1604: Nova Faelix Arabia*

ship. Each arch was a series of ratios, the result of reflections which depended directly or indirectly on the Pythagorean-Platonic division of the musical scale. The first arch was of the Tuscan order, 'being the principal pillar of those 5. upon which the *Noble Frame of Architecture* doth stand'. Such arches were visual statements on the new King's reign with their governing principles of order, harmony and concord. Ben Jonson paraphrases Alberti, who is in turn paraphrasing Vitruvius, in defining these concepts:

> The nature and propertie of these Deuices being, to present alwaies some one entire bodie, or figure, consisting of distinct members, and each of those expressing it selfe, in their owne actiue sphere, yet all, with that generall harmonie so connexed, and disposed, as no one little part can be missing to the illustration of the whole. …

In this Jonson ironically gives voice to one of the key principles upon which Inigo Jones based his whole philosophy not only for architecture but for the court fêtes of the Stuart kings.

This vast development in the techniques of spectacle in the service of the State during the sixteenth century in the way of painted sets, machinery and the control of light was also entirely consonant with certain lines of thought in relation to dramatic theory. The basis for the Renaissance theory of spectacle was Aristotle, who defined the purpose of drama as to produce a sense of wonder in the mind of the spectator. Vitruvius, writing of the classical theatre, praised stage machinery which gave pleasure to the onlooker. These two attitudes were linked by Serlio, who combined Aristotle's theory of wonder with Vitruvian stage spectacle, going straight into a discourse at some length on the marvels of elaborate scenic effects which leave, he says, 'many beholders abashed'. Such creations too, he writes, are the outward expression of the magnanimity and liberality of princes: 'The more such things cost, the more they are esteemed, for they are things which stately and great persons doe, which are enemies to niggardlinesse.' 'This is it,' writes Ben Jonson in his turn, 'hath made the most royal princes and greatest persons, who are commonly the personators of these actions .... studious of riches and magnificence in the outward celebration or show, which rightly becomes them.'

Magnificence was thus an element of fundamental importance to the Renaissance and Baroque court. This exultation of vast prodigal expenditure as a virtue came through a humanist revival of a Thomist–Aristotelian philosophical position. The praise of magnificence arose through the defence by Florentine humanists of the building projects of Cosimo il Vecchio. In doing this they looked first to St Thomas, who had classified magnificence as a virtue, and through him to Aristotle who, in the *Nicomachean Ethics*, is even more precise: '... great expenditure is becoming to those who have suitable means to start with, acquired by their own efforts or from ancestors or connexions, and to people of high birth and reputation, and so on; for all these things bring with them greatness and prestige.' Magnificence thus became a princely virtue. A prince must be seen to live magnificently, to dress splendidly, to furnish his palaces richly, to build sumptuously or to send grand embassies to other monarchs. No other philosophy could otherwise explain the vast sums of money expended by Henry VIII on the Field of Cloth of Gold, Mary of Hungary on the fêtes at Binche, or Catherine de'Medici on her sets of 'magnificences'. In the case of a Catherine de'Medici or a Charles I, the importance of court spectacle as a demonstration of regal 'magnificence' was such that their greatest artistic creations came during a time when the Crown was not only bankrupt but heavily in debt. This gives some measure of the significance attached to the court fête during the sixteenth and seventeenth centuries.

The central development to occur under princely auspices during the sixteenth century is the emergence of the illusionistic stage. As the century draws to its close the preference is more and more for indoor spectacles where visual effects can be more easily controlled, where the eyes of the spectator can be almost forced to look at things in a certain way. And by the end of the century that certain way was single point perspective. The discoveries of scientific perspective, applied since the middle of the fifteenth century to painting, was, in its turn, applied to court spectacle. In the case of a single painting, once the onlooker had learnt the rules of how to look, that converging lines meant distance, that things got smaller the further away they were, it seemed a perfectly reasonable way of looking at a painted area of panel or canvas immediately before one's eyes. Transferred to court spectacle it was much less satisfactory. The old–established means of décor in the form of scattered props and moveable pageant cars enabled everyone placed round the three sides of a hall to take part in the visual experience. In contrast, a stage with a proscenium arch, side wings and painted backcloth was viewable in perfection from one point only, for all the lines of perspective met in the eyes of the onlooking prince. Those sitting at the sides of the arena saw nothing but distorted scenery. In court spectacle perspective stage sets were the ultimate apotheosis of the monarch, for they deliberately added to the other hierarchical gradations increasingly governing court life, that of sight. The more important one was, the closer one sat to the king, and the closer one was to the king, the nearer one's eyes were to reading the unfolding spectacle with his eyes. The promotion and spread of this type of illusion, which was established as the norm by the fourth decade of the seventeenth century, is directly connected with the rise of absolutism. In France it was Cardinal Mazarin, an arch–creator of the absolute monarch, who used the Italian scenographer Giacomo Torelli to manufacture perspective stage sets in which the newly tamed nobility were to take part in the ritual *ballets de cour* in honour of the king. In England it was Inigo Jones who firmly introduced, even though his aristocratic audience took twenty years to comprehend it, perspective

63 Van Lochem,
*The 'Salle du
Palais Cardinal'*

stage scenery two years after the accession of a monarch who believed in and was the foremost exponent of the theory of the Divine Right of Kings.

If one had to define the Renaissance court fête in relation to the prince, one would say that its fundamental objective was power conceived as art. The fête enabled the ruler and his court to assimilate themselves momentarily to their heroic exemplars. For a time they actually became the 'ideas' of which they were but terrestrial reflections. The world of the court fête is an ideal one in which nature, ordered and controlled, has all dangerous potentialities removed. In the court festival the Renaissance belief in man's ability to control his own destiny and harness the natural resources of the universe find their most extreme assertion. In their astounding transformations, which defeat magic, defy time and gravity, evoke and dispel the seasons, banish darkness and summon light, draw down even the very influences of the stars from the heavens, they celebrate man's total comprehension of the laws of nature. The Renaissance court fête in its fullness of artistic creation was a ritual in which society affirmed its wisdom and asserted its control over the world and its destiny.

V *Francis I's Entry into Lyon, 1515:*

ABOVE LEFT a. *The Baptism of Clovis with St Rémy, St Vaast, Noble Assistance and a gentlewoman of arms*

b. *Fleur de lys bearing Francis I flanked by Grâce de Dieu and France. Lyon and Loyalty stand at the foot*

BELOW c. *Francis I guides the Ship of France drawn by the White Hind*

64 *Festival at Binche, 1549. The Banquet in
the Enchanted Chamber*

3 Images of Empire

THE EMPEROR CHARLES V

On 29 June 1539 Eleanora of Toledo, daughter of the Viceroy of Naples, made her solemn entry into the city of Florence as its future Duchess. The bride was the choice of the Emperor Charles V, and the most important of the triumphal arches to greet her on arrival was one in his honour. The procession paused to admire an elaborate arch over which could be seen the figure of Charles himself, arrayed *à l'antique*, crowned with laurel and carrying the imperial sceptre, river gods at his feet, flanked, to his right, by the figures of Spain and New Mexico, followed by Neptune, to show 'that the Western Ocean is dominated by His Majesty', while, to the left, stood Germany, with shield and lance, together with Italy and Africa. This formidable array had beneath it the following inscription: AUGUSTUS CAESAR DIVUM GENS AUREA CONDIT SAECULA ('Augustus Caesar, the offspring of gods, founds a Golden Age'), a tag taken from the famous prophecy of imperial greatness in Book Six of the *Aeneid*. Such tableaux of imperial grandeur, enhanced by the forms of Renaissance classicism, were to be re-enacted all over Europe in the first half of the sixteenth century, not only within Charles's own vast dominions, but both in England and in France. By his abdication in 1556 every educated person within Europe must have been familiar with the rhetoric and imagery of sacred empire.

65 After Parmigianino, *Charles V, 1530*

66 *Column 'impresa' of Charles V*

It was ironical that the art of festival was to give its most exuberant expression in the first half of the sixteenth century less to nascent nationalism than to glorifying a dramatic and unexpected revival of the phantom of universal empire. The Emperor Charles V ruled over domains of a richness and greatness beyond the dreams of the Romans. From his paternal grandfather, the Emperor Maximilian, came the hereditary Habsburg lands within the Empire; from his paternal grandmother, those within the area of the Low Countries, once ruled by the Dukes of Burgundy; from his maternal grandparents, a united Spain. To these Charles was to add in 1519 the title of Holy Roman Emperor, and territorially, by conquest, war or discovery, most of Italy and the New World. His vast domains came to be symbolized by his personal *impresa* of the two columns of Hercules, boundaries of the antique world, and the motto *Plus Ultra*.

Through his own relentless policy of dynastic aggrandizement, most of the remainder of Europe came within his orbit by marriage at one time or another, from Denmark to Milan, from Hungary to England. During his lifetime Charles defeated and captured his rival, Francis I, at the Battle of Pavia in 1525, and two years later imperial troops sacked Rome. In the years following it seemed as though the whole known world was subject

66

80

to One, and One who had not only been crowned by the Pope but had taken the faith to the New World, had defeated the Infidel and seemed on the brink of resuming imperial 'rights' by summoning a general council to reform the Church and end the Lutheran schism.

Charles V's fêtes were, therefore, great compilations of imperial mythology: globes of the world, images of the cosmos, gods and goddesses, heroes and heroines, subject peoples, held together by Latin tags from authors celebrating Augustan grandeur. In short, the revival of empire represented in the figure of the Emperor Charles V enabled Renaissance humanists and artists to apply to a living individual the whole rediscovered repertory of classical antiquity. As the inheritor of sacred empire, the use of classical architectural motifs and the re-creation of imperial triumphs in his honour have a meaning beyond that of mere empty rhetoric. In order to understand something of the richness of that meaning, it is necessary to grasp at least in rudimentary form the heritage of imperial ideas as it stood at the opening of the sixteenth century in Europe.

The Roman Empire of classical antiquity had ended over a thousand years before, in 476, on the death of Romulus Augustulus, and with him the reality of empire vanished in western Europe, although its idea remained. Ideas of universal empire, of the sacred rule of the One over the whole world, were essentially Hellenistic, taken over by the Romans who developed and expanded the notions of *orbis terrarum* and *imperium* as forces giving peace, order and justice to the whole of humanity. This imperial mission to mankind was reinforced when the Empire became Christian, thus identifying itself with the aims of a universal religion. The reign of the Emperor Augustus became sanctified in retrospect because it was at that time, imperial theorists argued, that Christ had chosen to be born. The righteousness of imperial rule was acknowledged by Christ himself, they claimed, when, on being shown a coin bearing the profile of Caesar, he said: 'Render unto Caesar the things which are Caesar's; and unto God the things that are God's.' The pagan Empire was further enhanced by Sybilline pronouncements: Virgil's *Fourth Eclogue*, with its famous prognostication of the birth of a child who would inaugurate a new era of universal peace and restore the Age of Gold, epitomized in the return of the maiden Justice or Astraea to earth, was glossed as referring to the birth of Christ. The casting of Virgil in this role of Christian prophet meant that the whole pagan rhetoric of the Golden Age could thus be taken over and used within the context of Christian imperial mythology. Historiographically the position of the Empire was recast by St Augustine and Orosius within an eschatological framework crystallized in the doctrine of the Four Monarchies, one which still carried force in the sixteenth century. These were the Assyrian, Babylonian, Greek and Roman, which spanned human history and the last of which alone held at bay the advent of Antichrist. As long as the Empire remained, the day of Antichrist would not dawn.

The medieval Empire, stemming from the papal coronation of Charlemagne in 800, inherited all these strands, but as a result the imperial image was feudalized. The *imperator* was also a *chevalier*, a Christian knight, hero of sagas of romance. In the papal theory of empire the Emperor duplicated the role of the Pope in the temporal sphere. The popes claimed to wield both the temporal and the spiritual swords but had delegated the former to the Emperor to wield on behalf of the Church. This was the theoretical position maintained by the Pope, while imperialists later claimed that the Emperor received his sword direct from Christ, and, moreover, that he had certain powers within the Church, notably the right to summon general councils. The Middle Ages were rent by the terrible struggles of Pope and Emperor and by the close of the fifteenth century the Empire had been reduced to little more than a localized area within Germany. It still had its theoretical exponents and dreamers of *renovatio*, notably Dante, whose treatise *De Monarchia* draws together in convenient form the classic arguments for the universal rule of the One based on cosmological, theological and philosophical grounds.

At the opening of the sixteenth century and the consolidation of power by the Habsburg, Valois and Tudor dynasties, nothing seemed further from political reality than an imperial *renovatio*. With Charles V, however, the Empire suddenly became a fact overnight. For almost forty years the mythology of universal empire ran riot in relation to Charles V, having a profound effect on the development of the mythologies of the national monarchies. For Charles the revival of sacred empire was enhanced by its coincidence with the spread of the Renaissance style *à l'antique*. More vividly than any emperor since antiquity was Charles depicted as a Roman *imperator* in antique armour, his brow wreathed in laurel. To his court, moreover, were attached notable exponents of the theories of sacred empire. The imperial chancellor, Mecurino Gattinara, was one whose ideas stemmed from Dante's *De Monarchia* and who fervently supported the expansion of Charles's dominions to embrace new horizons. Another was the court preacher and historiographer, Antonio Guevara, whose book *The Dial of Princes* had a European influence and who repeated, amid a disquisition on imperial and royal virtues, the arguments that the rule of the One over the whole world is best. A third was the Emperor's Latin secretary, Alfonso de Valdés, who wrote, following the sack of Rome, a *Dialogue of Lactantio and an Archdeacon*, drawing on medieval defenders of imperial rights against papal encroachments and fusing them with attitudes which were Erasmian. In this treatise the notorious sack was cast as a divine judgement, papal shame opening the way to the Emperor asserting his right to summon a general council which would end the Lutheran schism and inaugurate ecclesiastical reform. Charles never actually wielded these powers, but for almost half a century he remained the focal point for those who believed that he would.

To the ethos of imperial myths and sagas revived can be added another ingredient. Three years before the spectacular *renovatio* of empire embodied in the imperial election of 1519, Erasmus dedicated a book to Charles which had a profound influence on the idea of monarchy throughout Europe. The *Institution of a Christian Prince* recasts for the Christian humanist the medieval *speculum principis* tradition. The ideal prince was one who had received such a Christian and humanist education. The heroes and heroines whose virtues he should pattern himself upon figure in the classical texts beloved by Renaissance humanists, in Plato, Cicero, Seneca and Plutarch. Educated in this manner princes would be animated to act in concert and advance universal peace. The ideas embodied in this text find very vivid expression in the State entries staged not only for the Emperor Charles V but for monarchs throughout Europe, where time and again figures representing the princely virtues were paraded for their contemplation, and where examples of virtuous behaviour from antiquity were acted out, painted or sculpted for their edification.

In the moving speech that the Emperor made at his abdication, he recalled to those present his peregrinations: ten times to the Low Countries, nine to Germany, seven to Italy, six to Spain, four times through France, twice into England and twice to Africa. This list alone conveys the supranational character of imperial rule besides the geographical extent of his universal monarchy. It focuses attention too on the ceremonial progress as a political weapon in the hands of monarchs during the sixteenth century. Progresses

67 *Procession for Charles V's Entry into Bologna, 1529*

consolidated support for a régime, popularized its attitudes, took them down to the roots of local government, and made concrete the abstract of the Crown in the actual presence of the ruler. The sixteenth century was an age of royal progresses. Charles V was not alone in using this as a means of furthering dynastic power and focusing loyalty to the Crown. Catherine de'Medici also knew the value of the ceremonial progress. In the pause that followed the first of the religious wars Charles IX was taken on a long tour of his dominions, the *'Grand Voyage de France'*, making formal entries into each of his major cities and framing the journey with two great series of 'magnificences', at Fontainebleau in 1564 and at Bayonne on the Spanish frontier the year after. The most legendary and most successful of all these exponents of the royal progress was Queen Elizabeth I. These endless peregrinations, which were so often the despair of her ministers, were the means by which the cult of the imperial virgin was systematically promoted.

   As a prologue to the festivals of the progresses of Charles V, however, comes the most significant spectacle of the reign, the coronation of the Emperor at Bologna in 1530. This event represented the climax of imperial ambitions ever since Charles had been crowned King of the Romans at Aix-la-Chapelle on 23 October 1520 and had asked the German princes for men and money to reopen the Italian wars and achieve an imperial coronation in Rome. The coronation was the outcome of long years of conflict between Charles and Francis I in Italy. In 1525 Francis I was de-

feated and captured at the Battle of Pavia and by the Treaty of Madrid agreed to abandon all French claims to Naples and Milan. Milan became an imperial fief and Naples was annexed to the Spanish Crown. No sooner was the French King released than he disclaimed the treaty as having been made under duress and, much to the embarrassment of the Emperor, concluded the Holy League of Cognac with Pope Clement VII, Florence and Venice on 24 May 1526. The imperial troops crossed the Alps and laid siege to Bologna, and the Pope, fearing the worst, made a treaty with Charles on 15 March, but all to no avail, for the army, undisciplined and unpaid, moved south and laid siege to Rome. The infamous sack of Rome, unwanted by Charles, placed the Pope virtually in imperial hands, although he subsequently escaped, first to Orvieto and subsequently to Viterbo. Once more a French army entered Italy, to be finally routed at Landriano on 21 June 1529. On 29 June Pope and Emperor signed the Treaty of Barcelona, ostensibly motivated by the need to unite against the Turk in Hungary. In this Charles recognized papal claims to Ravenna, Cervia, Modena, Reggio and Rubeira, and, in return, Charles was invested with the kingdom of Naples. Both were to unite against heresy, and the Pope threatened excommunication against those who allied themselves with the Turk. Meanwhile the Emperor's aunt, Margaret of Austria, Regent of the Netherlands, had negotiated a peace with the French King through his mother, Louise of Savoy. The result was the Ladies' Peace of Cambrai, signed on 3 August 1529. By this the Emperor renounced his

claims to the lost Burgundian lands and Francis, in turn, recognized Charles's right to Flanders and Artois and himself abandoned claims to Milan, Genoa and Naples. As a finishing touch, the Emperor's sister, Eleanor, was to marry Francis I, and as part of this universal peace Clement VII was to crown the Emperor. Late in July 1529 Charles left Barcelona for Italy and on 5 November made his solemn entry into Bologna.

67–70   The procession itself was a formidable demonstration of imperial power. All imperial processions were deliberately stage-managed to demonstrate the multi-nationality of Charles's domains. The Emperor was met at the Porta San Felice by twenty cardinals attended by four hundred papal guards. The cardinals dismounted from their mules and saluted his imperial majesty courteously. Three hundred light horsemen opened the imperial procession, followed by a troop of Spanish lords bearing banners and standards. Next came three hundred knights in armour with red plumes nodding in their helmets. Ten great cannon mounted on chariots were wheeled through the streets ahead of fourteen companies of German *Landsknechts* playing fife and tabour with huge banners fluttering in the wind. Two lords on horseback carried the imperial and the Burgundian standards, one the outspread eagle, the other a red cross of St Andrew on a white ground. Squadrons bearing ordnance followed, together with the German cavalry, culminating in a group of Spanish grandees surrounded by a hundred of the Emperor's personal bodyguard carrying halberds. Before Charles rode the Grand Marshal supporting the imperial sword,

68 *Procession for Charles V's Entry into Bologna, 1529*

while the Emperor himself was in complete armour with a golden eagle
on his helmet, bearing a sceptre in his hand, his horse caparisons of cloth
of gold embroidered with jewels. Four knights on foot supported a magnificent canopy over his head, eight pages attended him, and he was accompanied by Cardinals Farnese and Ancona.

At the city gate Charles kissed the cross proffered him, while the imperial heralds casually tossed eight thousand ducats in gold and silver to the
crowd. The Pope, surrounded by the entire papal court, waited to greet
him in the church of St Petronius. Charles travelled by a route which was
decorated with arches that symbolically spelt out the role of emperor as it
was conceived by the Pope in 1529. Visually the décor was entirely *à
l'antique*. This was the first time that the equation of Renaissance classical
detail and revived Roman imperialism had been made so completely. The
Porta San Felice was adorned with putti dancing and playing instruments joyful at the Emperor's coming. There was a triumph of Bacchus
with nymphs, fauns and satyrs, and one of Neptune with tritons, sirens and
sea-horses to express the idea that Charles's sway extended over both land
and sea. The town gate bore medallions of Caesar, Augustus, Vespasian
and Trajan, and equestrian statues of Camillus and Scipio Africanus with
effigies of other Romans famous as virtuous warriors and exemplars of
the virtue of prudence. Two Latin inscriptions promised even greater glory
to an Emperor who combined the qualities of such heroes with those of
being a champion of the Faith and a shield of Holy Church.

OVERLEAF
VI *Henry II's Entry into
Rouen, 1550*

87

LEFT AND RIGHT 69 and 70 *Procession fo*
Charles V's Entry into Bologna, 1529

BELOW 71   *The Coronation Cavalcade o*
Charles V and Clement VII, 1530

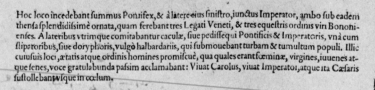

Hoc loco incedebant summus Pontifex, & à latere eius siniftro, junctus Imperator, ambo sub eadem thensa splendidißimè ornata, quam ferebant tres Legati Veneti, & tres equestris ordinis viri Bononienses. A lateribus vtrimque comitabantur caculæ, siue pedissequi Pontificis & Imperatoris, vnà cum stipatoribus, siue doryphoris, vulgò halbardariis, qui submouebant turbam & tumultum populi. Illic cuiusuis loci, ætatis atque ordinis homines promiscuè, qua quales erant fœminæ, virgines, iuuenes atque senes, voce gratulabunda passim acclamabant: Viuat Carolus, viuat Imperator, atque ita Cæsaris suftollebant vsque in cœlum.

Il Marchese d'Astorga, con dieci altri Baroni, tuui armati

The route was adorned with two further arches in the Doric style which carried numerous scenes and effigies reminding Charles of those emperors who had been protectors of the Holy See and defenders of the Faith. There were statues of Charlemagne, the Emperor Sigismund, Ferdinand of Aragon and Constantine, scenes from whose life included him presenting the imperial crown and sceptre to Pope Sylvester. These were rulers zealous in the Faith, active against heresy, the Jews and the Moors, extending the Church into new worlds. In this way the Pope defined the imperial role as the Emperor advanced through the streets of Bologna. Charles, the heir of the Caesars, was to be the perfect medieval emperor, whose sword and sceptre were at the service of the Pope. In its rigid insistence on the active propagation of the Faith, and on the destruction of heresy, it yet anticipates the themes of counter-reform. Charles was cast in the role of the virtuous young Emperor who had offended the spiritual power and devastated Italy, but who yet now humbly waited to make amends by submitting to Holy Church. The creation of Charles as the Champion of Christendom was played out in a final spectacle, the imperial coronation, on 24 February 1530, in a ceremony rich in symbolic statements on the subservience of *imperium* to *sacerdotium*. There was yet another, perhaps even more splendid procession, and further triumphal arches. On that day there was the unique sight of Charles riding at the Pope's right hand as the living embodiment of the dependence of *regnum* on *sacerdotium*.

71

91

Charles V's Entry into Messina, 1535:
72 Polidoro da Caravaggio, *Design
for the Arch at the Ponte della Dogana*

RIGHT 73 Polidoro da Caravaggio, *Decoration with the imperial arms*

For ten years the Emperor had wanted to visit his kingdoms of Sicily and Naples. This he now planned to do as an aftermath to a campaign against Barbarossa and the Turks in North Africa. On 10 June 1535 a vast fleet of Portuguese and Spanish galleys, the Genoese fleet under Andrea Doria, German contingents, other Italian and papal troops and Maltese set sail for Africa. Five days later they rode anchor at Carthage. The first object of Charles's attack was the fortress of La Goletta, which was stormed and taken with the whole of Barbarossa's fleet. Charles advanced on Tunis, where Christian slaves had seized the town in his name and into which he entered as victor. On 17 August he put to sea again and on the twenty-second he landed in his kingdom of Sicily.

Vasari's *Vite* are full of references to the vast preparations made for the reception of Charles V on his triumphal progress: '*Tornando sua Maestà dall'impresa d'Africa vittorioso, passò a Messina e dipoi a Napoli, Roma e finalmente a Siena.*'★ His progress actually ended on 28 April 1536, when he made his solemn entry into Florence. Italian and in particular Florentine artists, who specialized in such *apparati*, moved from one city to another ahead of the Emperor, working at frenetic speed in wood, paint and stucco to raise temporary decorations with which to receive him. Vasari records that the entry into Messina was designed by Polidoro da Caravaggio who '*fece archi trionfali bellissimi*',† although the text describing the occasion

72, 73

★ 'His Majesty, returning victorious from the capture of Africa, passed through Messina and then on to Naples, Rome and finally Siena.'
† '... made very fine triumphal arches.'

makes it clear that the main feature was the extraordinary chariots that preceded the imperial cortège to the cathedral. On one six Moors were bound prisoner at the foot of an altar laden with trophies, on the second, larger car stood the four cardinal Virtues, while angels revolved two hemispheres bearing the constellations. Above, a globe of the world turned, on which there stood the Emperor crowned and bearing a victory in his hand. When the procession reached the cathedral the chariot carrying the prisoners stopped before the door from above which floated down twenty-four winged angels from a starry sky, who gathered up the trophies from the altar and ascended with them heavenward singing the Emperor's praises. These visions of a crusading emperor were elaborated at a solemn mass the next day. Suspended above the nave of the cathedral was a model of Constantinople with the Turkish arms over it. After the Gospel had been read an amazed congregation saw an imperial eagle soar through the air and lead an attack on the city in the middle of which, when the Turkish arms had been vanquished, a cross suddenly appeared.

A month later, on 25 November, Charles entered Naples. The main feature of the Neapolitan entry was the series of *colossi*, over-life-sized statues. Piero Valeriano in his *Hieroglyphica* explains that famous men of antiquity were honoured by statues whose dimensions matched their merit. The *colossi* were prototypes of imperial grandeur or tributes to it: Jove wielding sceptre and thunderbolt, Victory proffering branches of oak and palm, Atlas sustaining the world, Hercules with the imperial columns, Mars, Fame and Faith. Here, for the first time, the Emperor's Turkish victories were acclaimed in a series of canvases decorating a triumphal arch. The historical parallels which the taking of La Goletta and Tunis and the flight of Barbarossa evoked were humanist ones of Scipio Africanus, Hannibal, Alexander the Great and Julius Caesar, and not those of medieval crusading rulers.

The new Pope, Paul III, a Farnese, bestowed on the Emperor a Roman imperial triumph, the route being that used in antiquity. It passed beneath the arches of Constantine, Titus and Septimus Severus, suitably refurbished with paintings and appropriate Latin inscriptions. Charles, it is recorded, was much moved by this and stopped and studied them. To these the Pope had added other temporary arches, notably at the Porta S. Sebastiano, where Battista Franco had executed great canvases of the Triumphs of Scipio Major and Minor hailing Charles as the *Tertio Africano*. But surpassing all was the one designed by Antonio di Sangallo

74

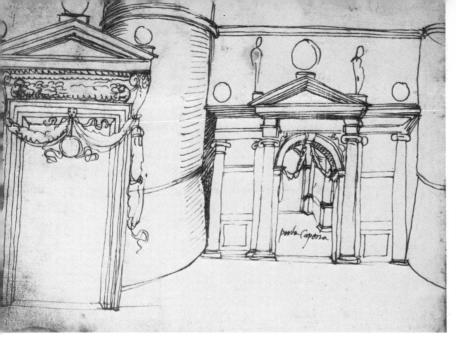

Charles V's Entry into Rome, 1536:
74 Arch at the Porta S. Sebastiano

75 Arch designed by Antonio di Sangallo
at the Palazzo di San Marco

at the Palazzo di San Marco. Vasari, whose career was so intimately bound up with providing *apparati* for the Medici, states that he had never seen a more superbly proportioned arch, which for its statues, paintings and other decorations deserved to rank among the wonders of the world. Sangallo had numerous artists working under him, including Francesco Salviati, who painted *storie di chiaroscuro*, and probably the young Flemish artist, Martin van Heemskerck. The arch was of the Corinthian order with silver pillars and golden capitals. On the top was the gigantic figure of Roma seated between the Emperor's ancestors, St Albert, the Emperors Maximilian, Frederick and Rudolf. The paintings depicted the taking of La Goletta and Tunis, the Emperor releasing Christian prisoners, being crowned King of Tunis, and other allegories of the campaign.

Baccio da Montelupo, who had executed fourteen stucco statues for the Ponte di S. Angelo, meanwhile rushed ahead to Florence, whither the imperial court made its way via Siena. Until 1552 the latter managed to maintain its independence as one of the few remaining republican states in Italy, and although it accorded a welcome to the Emperor and his personal retinue the city refused to allow the army within its gates. The citizens of Siena had expected Charles some six years before and in readiness had commissioned an equestrian statue by Domenico Beccafumi. This was now brought into use and met the Emperor at the city gate. The statue was of gold and the Emperor was shown in antique dress, enemies being trampled beneath his horse's hooves. Beccafumi had designed a castle for it to stand on, which was wheeled in the actual procession to the Palazzo Signoria.

95

Four days later Charles entered Florence. Alessandro de'Medici, whose family Charles had restored to power, had already written from Naples giving instructions for the most sumptuous of entertainments to be prepared. Under the direction of a committee, a team of artists and sculptors, including Vasari, accorded the Emperor his most splendid entry yet. At the Porta di S. Piero Gattolini, where the two imperial columns formed an archway, Charles was met by the Archbishop of Florence. Along the route there was a statue of *Allegrezza* by Montorsoli, the obligatory arches covered with paintings of the recent imperial victories, a silver Hercules, a Jason bearing the golden fleece (referring to the Order of the Golden Fleece of which Charles was sovereign), and the figures of *Pax* and *Victoria Augusti*. In answer to Siena there was to have been an equestrian statue of Charles, but being unfinished the horse alone was put on display in the Piazza S. Trinità and dedicated to the '*imperatori Carolo Augusto victorissimi*'. In a blaze of glory the imperial progress drew to its close.

In these entries, following in the train of the one into Bologna for his coronation in 1530, the powers of universal empire, of a reborn Augustus Caesar, are fully celebrated in decoration based on the researches of Renaissance antiquarians. In the North, in the Low Countries or in Eng-

76 Vermeyen,
*Charles V as St James
Matamore*

77 *Charles V's Entry into Milan, 1541. Triumphal Arch*

78 Titian, *Charles V on Horseback*

land, the royal entry remained a dialogue between the prince and his subjects paying homage but respectfully reminding him of the virtues he should cultivate and the liberties of his subjects that he should respect. The visual mythology of the Italian entries is that of total subservience to a supreme power, a *Dominus Mundi*. Such visions were enhanced by the use of the whole rediscovered repertory of Renaissance classicism. There are no *tableaux vivants*, except in Sicily, but mock antique arches of wood painted as marble and stone, gold and silver, on to which were placed cameo paintings together with stucco and plaster statues. Charles is always the Roman Emperor, crowned with laurel, his victories celebrated as emulating those recorded by Livy. Such décor for princes was part of the rhetoric of the Renaissance court artist, whose role was to elaborate, under direction, the mythology of a ruling dynasty. Unlike the North there are no allusions to knightly chivalry, only to the *imperator*; the victories are of valiant Romans over Carthaginians, not invading knights over infidel Turks. Attitudes are epitomized in the introduction of that most significant of imperial images, the equestrian statue. This was an honour reserved in antiquity for the Emperor alone. Four years later, in 1541, the theme was repeated in Milan and its final form was Titian's great canvas celebrating the defeat of the Lutherans at the Battle of Mühlberg. Unlike his fellow countrymen, Titian sensitively manages to fuse classical allusion with traditions of northern heroic chivalry.

97

Charles had been absent from the Low Countries since 1531. Led by discontent in Ghent due to economic depression, the whole province of Artois was in a state of latent revolt by the summer of 1539. During one of those periodic lulls in the endless struggle of Habsburg and Valois, Francis I offered the Emperor passage through his own dominions and ordered that all possible honour be paid to him. Travelling through France by way of Bayonne and Bordeaux to Poitiers, Charles passed northwards into the Loire district to be met by an ageing Francis. Great fêtes were staged at Fontainebleau at Christmas, when the Emperor was once more shortly reunited with his sister, Eleanor, and in January Charles continued his journey by way of Paris towards Chantilly, Soissons, Saint-Quentin, to Valenciennes and Cambrai. By the end of January 1540 Charles was in Brussels. The vengeance wreaked on the rebels in Ghent was savage: their privileges were plucked from them, the city fathers were condemned to walk in procession barefoot with halters round their necks to beg the imperial pardon, and a vast fortress was built to control the town.

In comparison with the Italian *trionfi* of four years before, the French entries are medieval and one moves back in time to an earlier era. At Poitiers there were *'certains théâtres et mystères moraulx et historiaulx'*.★ The university neatly solved the problems raised by the visit by building a triumphal arch from which hung a crown seven or eight feet in diameter with the imperial arms to one side, the French to the other and the university's between. Beneath the imperial arm stood *Honor Maiestatis*, beneath the French, *Maiestatis Honor*, while between *Unitas* bore up the crown. Further along the route there was a fountain on which stood Peace with red and white wine spurting from either breast, while below, France held the King's device of the salamander and Germany a phoenix, the device of Charles's sister, the French Queen Eleanor. The city of Orléans dodged the issue altogether by refusing to include any devices or inscriptions for fear of giving offence. The Paris entry had two pageants and three triumphal arches, one of which was *à l'antique*. In the first there was an orchard surrounded by mountains with, on one side, a fortress with a door locked and bolted – the Gate of War. Opposite, the Gate of Peace was open, with the badges of the Order of St Michael and the Golden Fleece above it, which the monarchs had exchanged shortly before at Aigues-Mortes. In front of the Gate of Peace stood a beautiful girl called Alliance.

★ 'A number of theatres and moral and historical mystery plays.'

In the second pageant two eagles with outspread wings held in their claws an asp and a basilisk, a lion and a dragon, while in the clouds above Divine Will held a banderole with the legend from Psalm 91: *super aspidem et basilicum ambulabis* and *Et conculcabis leonem et draconem*. Below these stood three figures taken from Alciati's *Emblemata*: Accord with her hive of bees, Discord bearing fire and water and, between the two, Peace seated on a throne *à l'antique* bearing her branch of olive. The city further presented Charles with a candelabra of silver depicting Hercules bearing his two columns and the mottoes: *Plus Oultre* and *Altera alterius*. The medievalism of this entry was repeated in provincial form at Valenciennes, where Charles was saluted by the Theological Virtues, by David and Jonathan as prototypes of the friendship of Charles and Francis, by a meeting of Pity and Truth, Peace and Justice, who embraced as described in the psalm while the Three Graces awarded the accolade to the Emperor.

The theme of the entries is that of the harmony of princes in the practice of the virtues and the maintenance of peace. This journey of the Emperor across France in 1539 through lands ruled by a fellow prince was part of the ethos of the period, which was preoccupied in the ideology of its politics with notions of European concord and Universal Peace uniting Christian monarchs in action against the Turk. This found its most vivid and influential expression in Erasmus's *Querela Pacis*, published in 1517. In this Peace laments the folly of war and suggests that the only truly Christian method of settling international disputes was by means of discussion and arbitration. Universal harmony was now possible, concluded Peace, because the leading European princes desired peace. It is this notion of the concord of princes achieved through personal encounter which provides the thought context for some of the great confrontations of the century: the meeting of Henry VIII and Francis I at the Field of Cloth of Gold in 1520; the meeting of Charles V and Francis I at Aigues-Mortes in 1538; the projected encounter between Elizabeth I and Mary, Queen of Scots, at York in 1566, and the conference at Bayonne between Catherine de'Medici and her daughter, the Queen of Spain, in 1565. All these were animated by the notion that European peace could be secured by fraternal gatherings of monarchs, and nearly all were the occasions for the most staggering manifestations of princely magnificence. All were politically disastrous.

OPPOSITE VII *Tournament
ceremonial from Réné of Anjou's
'Traité de la forme et devis d'un
tournois':
ABOVE a. *Knights engaging
in combat*
BELOW b. *The inspection of
helmets*

Ten years later, in 1549, came the most splendid series of fêtes of the whole reign, those held to mark the recognition of Charles's eldest son Philip as hereditary ruler of the Low Countries. During the intervening years the Emperor's universal policy had broken down. There had been a disastrous expedition against Algiers, another war with France and endless difficulties, both religious and political, within the Empire itself. After seeking a religious compromise between Catholics and Protestants, an effort doomed to failure due to the intransigence of the theologians, the Emperor finally took up arms on behalf of Catholicism and won a resounding victory over the Lutherans at Mühlberg in 1547. This was not a solution in any way to the religious differences rending his lands, and he still pressed hard for the Protestants to be heard during the opening sessions of the Council of Trent. The Low Countries' fêtes marked an important political decision on the future division of the Habsburg lands. Charles had finally decided that the Low Countries should henceforth be linked to Spain and that this should be secured within his own lifetime by the recognition by the Estates of his son as their ruler. This was linked to projects to be unrealized, that Philip was to be recognized as Emperor in succession to his father. Towards the close of 1548 Prince Philip, with a vast entourage in the manner of the old Dukes of Burgundy, landed in Italy and proceeded in triumph by way of Genoa, Milan, Mantua, Trent and up through Germany to the Low Countries.

Each town vied with the other in the splendour of its reception of the Prince. The progress through the Low Countries began in Brussels and continued by way of Louvain, Ghent, Bruges, Lille, Tournoi and subsequently the northern towns, but its climax was the most famous entry of the century, the one made into Antwerp on 10 September. The imagery of the entries was both biblical and classical. The relationship of Charles and Philip was acted out in the stories of Abraham making Isaac his heir, Joseph visiting Jacob, or Solomon crowned King of Israel at the behest of his father David. Classical prototypes were Philip of Macedon and Alexander the Great, Coelus Adrian succeeding Trajan, Priam choosing Hector or Flavius Vespasian attended by his son Titus. Everywhere the imperial descent was celebrated, everywhere the labours of Hercules expressed Charles's conquests by land and sea for Empire and Church, and everywhere the princely virtues, those Erasmian attributes of the Christian prince, were recommended for study by the heir apparent. The Ghent *entrée* was almost wholly based on an exposition of the cardinal virtues

Prince Philip's Entry into Antwerp, 1549 (80–4):
80 *The Genoese Arch*

79 *Prince Philip's Entry into Ghent, 1549. Arch with Charlemagne designating Louis the Pious as his heir*

and their virtuous subdivisions, while at Lille the mighty Ship of State was seen bearing Emperor and son towards the haven of the Temple of Felicity, manned by maidens as the Virtues. But the changing mood of the times found disturbing expression in tableaux of religion at Lille, where the themes of incipient counter-reform were manifest in a forthright statement. While Charles and Philip stood within the Temple of Virtue, below yawned a gaping hell-mouth inhabited by the figure of Martin Luther. Further on, the figure of the Catholic Church was to be seen treading Heresy underfoot, attended by Pope and Emperor as the shield of the faith, while nearby Luther and Zwingli rubbed shoulders with Julian the Apostate, Simon Magus, Arius and Huss, as vanquished heretics. The tableaux anticipated all that was to happen for the rest of the century.

Nothing, however, was apparently to eclipse the glory of the Antwerp entry. Its fame was European and illustrated texts were issued in Latin, French and Flemish. Vast armies of workmen laboured in raising arches and street pageants: 895 carpenters, 234 painters, 498 other workmen. The city itself, then at its apogee, employed 421 carpenters, 37 painters, 16 sculptors, 137 actors and 300 labourers. Amongst the foreign contributors, the Genoese excelled all in magnificence, spending some 9,000 florins on their arch, which took seventeen days to build and upon which 280 men worked. The Antwerp entry reflects in heightened form the themes of the other entries, the tension between wealthy cities with their ancient rights and liberties and the pressure of a dynasty wishing to centralize power.

81 *The Spanish Arch. The imperial
columns and the Temple of Janus*

82 *The Golden Age*

Ironically the official texts commemorating the event avoided printing
the truth, that in spite of all its magnificence the Antwerp entry was a
scaled-down celebration of a political failure. It had been planned to
welcome Philip as the next Emperor, but the refusal of the Electors to
grant Charles's wish meant that Philip entered Antwerp only as future
King of Spain and as Marquess of the Holy Roman Empire in Antwerp.
Many decorations were left unfinished, including a bridge with thirty-
foot-high obelisks and a round Temple of Victory outside the gate of St
George. When the programme for the street decorations is analysed, it is
possible to trace remnants of what was to have been the greatest imperial
fête of the century. In the arches and street pageants the realities of an
existing political situation were paraded before princely eyes. As of old the
citizens of Antwerp offered no slavish adulation of an absolute monarch,
as did their Italian contemporaries, but loyalty and service to one who re-
spected their ancient rights and privileges. The very acceptance of Philip
as their future sovereign within his father's lifetime was a novelty. Two or
three years earlier the Emperor had considered the possibility of making
the Low Countries into an independent kingdom and, as a first step, came
the recognition of Philip as heir. Mary of Hungary received ready support
from the states of Brabant and Malines but found those of Flanders
recalcitrant, so much so that Charles himself summoned their deputies to
Brussels. In order to achieve the pragmatic sanction whereby he could
unite his hereditary lands, he was forced to make concessions and recog-

83 *Charles V and Prince Philip bear up the world*

84 *God the Father crowns Prince Philip*

nize '*toutes les constitutions et tous les privilèges accordés anterieurement par les seigneurs aux divers territoires*'.★

This settlement, so rich in seeds of future discontent, was vividly portrayed in the Antwerp entry. Time and again Philip was reminded of the vast riches made from the freedom of its trade. On one pageant stood the god Mercury, protector of merchants, attended by Commerce together with the five nations who had communities within the city. On another, Peace stood with Liberty at her side. From these flowed Concord and Policy, whose hands stretched towards Ceres, together with Abundance and Money. The Latin inscription accompanying these figures began with the words *Dulcis libertas* and referred all blessings to this virtue. Another arch glorified *Moneta*, from which all human order and happiness flowed. In these *tableaux vivants* the young Prince was reminded by his future subjects of the conditions upon which their prosperity depended. Arches on the old imperial themes of ancestry, the Golden Age, world dominion, those depicting imperial victories and imperial *pax* and, above all, the final arch in which God the Father, standing before a huge revolving heaven, flanked by Virtues, invested Prince Philip with sceptre and sword and placed a jewelled crown on his head must have been bitter reminders to Philip that he was not Emperor elect.

★ '… all the constitutions and privileges granted earlier to the various lands by their rulers.'

85 *Festival at Binche, 1549. Wild-men interrupt a court ball and abduct ladies*

But the most spectacular and marvellous of all the fêtes that attended the recognition of Prince Philip as the Emperor's successor was given by the Queen Dowager, Mary of Hungary, at her palace at Binche. The setting was described by Brantôme as *'un miracle du monde'*, ('a wonder of the world') and the fêtes were on such a stupendous scale that they became proverbial: *Más brava que las fiestas de Bains* ('More splendid than the festivals of Binche'). Nearly all the entertainments were chivalrous in character. There was a foot combat in which knights arrived disguised as German pilgrims with their wives, only to find themselves rudely interrupted by the entry of knights dressed as huntsmen with their attendants letting live rabbits and cats loose in the enclosure. On another evening, wild-men interrupted the progress of a court ball to seize ladies and carry them off as prisoners to a nearby fortress which was stormed the following day. The Queen Dowager brought the fêtes to a close with a banquet in an Enchanted Room. A table descended in layers bearing sugared confections of extraordinary invention in vessels of glass and porcelain, while above was a ceiling across which the planets and stars moved and from which comfits and perfumes rained down upon the feasters. But the most significant event of all took place on 25 and 26 August and was entitled 'The Adventure of the Enchanted Sword and the *Château Ténébreux'*.

The preliminaries had taken place some time before in Ghent when, towards the close of a banquet, a grief-stricken knight had entered the hall and, throwing himself on his knees before the Emperor, had presented him with a letter and begged leave that he might fasten a cartel to the palace gate. The Emperor, having read the contents, gave permission for this to be done and said that he and his court would journey to Binche soon to see the strange things described in the missive. The court actually arrived on 22 August and two days after, during a court ball, another letter was delivered to Charles which was read to the assembled spectators. This was from the Knights Errant of Belgic Gaul, who begged the Emperor's assistance against an evil enchanter, Norabroch, who held various noble subjects of the Emperor prisoner in a castle, the *Château Ténébreux*, which he had further encircled with clouds so that it could not even be seen. The good Queen Fadade, however, had planted nearby the *Ile Heureuse*, out of which arose three huge columns that would ultimately bring about the magician's ruin. One was of jasper and in it a bejewelled sword was embedded, while the two others bore a prophecy: the knight who could draw forth the sword from the column would be the one who would break the evil spells, release the captives and destroy the *Château Ténébreux*. Such a knight would further be destined to succeed in other great enterprises which could not at the present be revealed. Before, however, any knight reached the *Ile Heureuse*, he must pass through three forms of combat: one at the barrier of the *Pas Fortuné* with the *Chevalier au Griffon Rouge*, and the second at the *Tour Périlleuse* with the *Chevalier à l'Aigle Noir*, and the third with the *Chevalier au Lion d'Or*. Knights who failed at any of these points of combat fell prey to the magician Norabroch. Those who passed all three boarded a boat like a dragon whose captain guided them to the *Ile Heureuse*, where they were to reveal their true identity. There each knight was to attempt to dislodge the sword. Those who failed withdrew honourably from the quest until a knight who answered the prophecy broke the enchantment. On hearing this dramatic saga the Prince and other knights of the court begged the Emperor that on the morrow they should be allowed to show their prowess.

The tournament lasted two days and the knights arrived in many disguises. There were Hungarian knights, there were knights of the Sun, of the Moon, of the Stars. There was the Knight of the White Rose and the Knight of Death. The last entered the arena surrounded by singers in black velvet chanting funerary responses. The tempo of the proceedings was enlivened from time to time by other effects: rain suddenly fell from the sky or there were terrible cries from the *Château Ténébreux*. Great was the joy of the captain of the dragon ship on the second day when the *Chevalier Ebré* withdrew the sword from the jasper column, but such happiness was short-lived when the prophecy revealed that it was a prince alone who would end the adventure of the enchanted sword. As evening drew on a knight called Beltenebros arrived. Having successfully completed the three combats he crossed to the island and withdrew the sword amid huge claps of thunder and hideous cries from the *Château*. When the knight informed the captain of his true identity, he fell on his knees in homage and then led the chosen knight to the far point of the island. Suddenly the clouds lifted, revealing the castle of Norabroch. It was reached by a bridge over which there was a gate firmly shut, on which hung a flask and before which were mustered the magician's knights. The chosen knight, armed with the enchanted sword, advanced over the bridge, vanquished the guards and smashed the flask, at which point the spell was immediately dissolved. The doors of the *Château* fell open, liberating the prisoners, who paid homage to their deliverer. Great was their joy when the knight revealed himself to be none other than Prince Philip.

It is useless to speculate as to whether or not Philip possessed the prowess to excel in this exercise of arms, because in the context of the symbolic import of the drama he had to be the victor. The entertainment drew for its nourishment on one of the deepest and most primitive of folklore motifs, that of the initiation ceremony. Themes such as these are woven inextricably into virtually every form of medieval romance: the mystery of the sacred sword which could only be drawn by the right person, an act followed by one of fealty or recognition. Such enactments are part of the pattern of European chivalrous literature, familiar to everyone in six-teenth-century Europe. The pseudonym, Beltenebros, chosen by Philip was taken from the *Amadis de Gaule,* a widely popular romance which contains most of the ingredients of the Binche fête. In theme and décor the tournament was an elaboration on those of the previous century, but developed and expanded to be more splendid than ever before. Old formulas and images applied to new situations were ever the material of the court fêtes. And in this case the political aims were clearly to present Prince Philip as the pre-ordained ruler of the Low Countries. Those present would be familiar with the difficulties encountered by both Emperor and aunt in getting the various Estates to accept Philip as their ruler before the Emperor's death. Away from the caveats of civic entertainments, with their concern for local liberties and privileges, in the milieu of the imperial court the statement could be made more forcefully. The Prince was un-compromisingly presented as a divinely ordained deliverer, defeating evil, breaking spells, through his valour alone rescuing the afflicted. Those who were to live through the next twenty years must have paused to reflect on the incredible optimism of pageantry.

The theme of the ruler as the deliverer, so highly developed within the context of chivalrous romance at Binche, was to be repeated again and again all over Europe in the late sixteenth and early seventeenth century. It had an enormous effect, for instance, on French court fêtes. In 1564 at Fontainebleau, where Catherine de'Medici staged the first of her sets of 'magnificences', Charles IX and his brother Anjou, as fulfillers of a pro-phecy concerning *'deux grands Princes'*, vanquished a giant and stormed an enchanted castle to release ladies. A year later this was reworked for the fêtes at Bayonne on the Spanish frontier. This time it was Charles IX alone who, as the promised knight who should banish spells and establish peace throughout Christendom, stormed past a giant and a dwarf into the spellbound castle. Catherine's youngest son organized an entertainment at the English court on the same lines in 1582. This time the magician's power could only be broken by the most excellent prince in the world, who happened to be most constant in the profession of his love to the most heroic and virtuous of princesses, that is, Queen Elizabeth I. In the case of a female monarch such as Elizabeth, the power of her virtues alone had force to dispel all charms. When she visited old Sir Henry Lee at Ditchley in the autumn of 1592 she penetrated an enchanted wood in which knights and ladies were imprisoned in the trees, entered a hall hung with charmed pictures, construed their meaning and thus broke the spell, causing her host to awaken from an enchanted slumber and those released from the wood to sing her praises:

> Happie houre, happie daie
> That Eliza came this waie.

The acting out by courtiers in dramatic form, in tournament, ballet and masque, of the Prince as the deliverer is one of the leitmotifs of the Renaissance court fête, investing crowned and anointed heads with apparently supernatural powers to banish magic and defeat forces of evil by the inherent strength of their royal virtues.

Although Binche develops a crucial theme in Renaissance festival dramatic denouement, its central tissue is the web of chivalrous romance spun round the imperial power. Chivalry was an international phenomenon and it was assiduously cultivated at the multinational court of Charles V. At Binche it is reflected in the nationalities of the knights who fought, who were Spanish, German, Flemish and Italian. It is caught time and again in the stage-management of processions for state entries, where detachments of imperial troops march in ceremonial order in their distinctive national costumes. Such supranationality was reflected in the fancy dresses worn in court entertainments. Imperial chivalry, however, found its most powerful format in the Order of the Golden Flecce, founded by Duke Philip the Good in 1430 out of his love of chivalry and his desire to protect Holy Church. To it belonged the highest nobility and leading councillors of the Emperor; from it sprang much of the imperial mythology concerning Jason and the Golden Fleece, which was repeated time without number whenever the Emperor was publicly celebrated. In spite of the multiplicity of their outward appearance, the subjects of Charles V were yet united in their knightly obedience to the imperial diadem.

86 *Charles V's Funeral Procession, 1558. Pageant Ship*

Almost a decade later, on 21 September 1558, two years after his abdication, the Emperor died in the monastic peace of Yuste. One final posthumous pageant sums up in retrospect the whole imperial saga. As part of the obsequies in Brussels on 29 December a great ship was solemnly drawn through the streets. Adorned with the arms of all the countries over which he had ruled, it was richly decorated with scenes and inscriptions recording the Emperor's triumphs. Before the central mast, on a stone labelled *Christus*, sat Faith bearing a cross, while Hope rode at the prow and Charity navigated from the helm. Behind arose the two imperial columns on rocks in the midst of the sea. In this way the imperial motto, '*Plus oultre*', now celebrated Charles's conquest of a heavenly kingdom. For the last time the pillars of Hercules and the ship of Jason and the Argonauts, the two heroes of the House of Burgundy, paid tribute to an emperor whose piety now carried him to greater glory in the world to come.

In an age of nascent nationalism and lingering universalism the imperial idea continued to have a tremendous appeal, particularly during the second half of the sixteenth century when the wars of religion gave rise to rulers becoming the focus for Messianic hopes. This becomes blended with streams of nationalist thought stemming from the assertion defining the position of the French kings in the later Middle Ages, that every monarch *est in patria sua imperator*, 'is emperor in his own land'. The arguments put forward by those defending these new national 'empires' drew heavily on the texts used to defend universal empire. In doing this they also drew to themselves the imperial mythology.

Imperial themes deriving from Charles V had an enormous impact on Elizabethan thought concerning the monarchy. The position taken up by the Crown in relation to the Church of being its governor and defender was based directly on the arguments used by those who had supported the Emperor against the Pope in the never-ending struggles during the Middle Ages. As the Pope had reduced the imperial power to nought, it was argued, his powers had devolved upon kings of individual countries. The famous Act in Restraint of Appeals of 1533, by which Henry VIII rejected papal authority, begins by stating that the realm of England was an 'empire' over which the Bishop of Rome had no authority. Bishop Jewel, the official apologist for the Anglican Settlement of 1559, sums up the position of the English Crown in the post-Reformation period exactly.

OPPOSITE 87 Attributed to Cornelius Ketel, *Elizabeth I as a Roman Vestal Virgin, c. 1580*

ELIZABETA D. G. ANGLIÆ. FRANCIÆ. HIBERNIÆ. ET VERGINIÆ
REGINA CHRISTIANAE FIDEI VNICVM PROPVGNACVLVM.

Immortalis honos Regum, cui non tulit ætas   *Queis ipse tantum superant reliqua omnia regna,*
Vlla prior, veniens nec feret vlla parem,   *Quantum tu maior Regibus es reliquis,*
Sospite quo nunquam terras habitare Britannas   *Viue precor felix tanti in moderamine regni,*
Desinet alma Quies, Iustitia atque Fides,   *Dum tibi Rex Regum cælica regna paret.*

In honorem serenissima sua celsitudinis hanc effigiem fieri curabat Ioannes Woutneelus belga. Anno 1596.

Whereas in olden times the Emperor had summoned Councils of the
Church, it was 'now a common right to all princes, forasmuch as kings are
now fully possessed in the several parts of the empire'. This formed the
politico-theological basis upon which the Tudors built up their position
as restorers of ancient purity to the polluted English Church by reassuming
the powers once rightfully enjoyed by emperors in the primitive Church.
The cult of Elizabeth I stems from this role as the just virgin of imperial
reform, descended from the ancient imperial house of Troy, the embodiment of the Tudor *pax* by virtue of the union of the two roses of York and

Lancaster. In her oft-sung role of Astraea, she is actually identified with the virgin of Virgil's *Fourth Eclogue*, whose advent foretells the Age of Gold and an imperial *renovatio*. Elizabeth reigns, in the words of the dedication of Edmund Spenser's epic *The Faerie Queene*, as the 'most high Mightie and Magnificent Empresse', whose 'empire' extends beyond the bounds of her tiny island kingdom to embrace the colony of Virginia.

The rhetoric of Golden Age falls fast round Elizabeth I. Gloriana, under which name Spenser celebrates the public aspect of his sovereign, is descended from the line of the Trojan Brutus, from whom spring kings and 'sacred Emperors'. In an imitation of Ariosto's prophecy in *Orlando Furioso* celebrating the empire of Charles V, Spenser uses Merlin to foretell the advent of the Tudor dynasty and in particular of an imperial virgin:

> Thenceforth, eternal union shall be made
> Between the nations different afore,
> And sacred Peace shall lovingly perswade
> The warlike minds, to learne her goodly lore,
> And ciuile armes to exercise no more;
> Then shall a royal virgin reign. ...

7
8

Occasional bursts of wild imperialism are part of the Eliza cult. It is glimpsed in the terrestrial globes that appear so frequently in her portraits, into one of which the crown of the Holy Roman Empire is even inserted. In direct reference to Charles V she is depicted, in the aftermath of the defeat of the mighty Armada, standing triumphant between the columns of the old imperial device. Like that of Charles V, too, Elizabethan imperialism draws to itself traditions of courtly chivalry, intensified in the case of Elizabeth I as she combined the twin aspects of sovereign and romantic heroine. At the Accession Day Tournament of 1590, the British *Virgo* and her growing empire found dramatic expression in the erection within the tiltyard of Whitehall Palace of the Temple of the Roman Vestal Virgins. Certain of the virgins bore to the Queen splendid gifts from the altar, while before the temple stood a by now familiar sight, a pillar bearing a crown embraced by an eglantine tree. On this hung a Latin prayer, ecstatic in its Eliza worship, stating that the Queen had moved one of the pillars of Hercules and that now her mighty empire stretched into the New World.

At the close of the century ideas of *renovatio* find their focus in Henry of Navarre, whose extraordinary career and conversion to Catholicism presaged to many a remarkable destiny. Humanist dreams of a solution to the

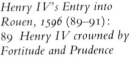

Henry IV's Entry into Rouen, 1596 (89–91):
89 Henry IV crowned by Fortitude and Prudence

89–91

divisions of Christendom, which had formerly found their nodal point in hoped-for actions by the Emperor Charles V, crystallize again around Henry IV. The French King's conversion to Catholicism, it was believed by many, opened the door to some universal religious solution. The French monarchy, as descendants themselves of sacred empire from Charlemagne and as guardians of Gallican liberties, had always attracted imperial mysticism. Even in the midst of the terrible war with the Catholic League, when it seemed that the French monarchy was about to slip into oblivion, the mythology of Charles V was revived in the imagery surrounding Henry IV. In the Rouen entry of 1596 the imperial columns appear, this time shattered at the King's feet, while he stands like an emperor astride a terrestrial globe. Prudence and Fortitude crowning him. At the turn of the century in the fêtes to welcome Marie de'Medici as the new Queen of France, the myth of imperial destiny is intensified. Echoing the

116

90 *An angel delivers a sword to Henry IV*

BELOW 91 *Naval Battle*

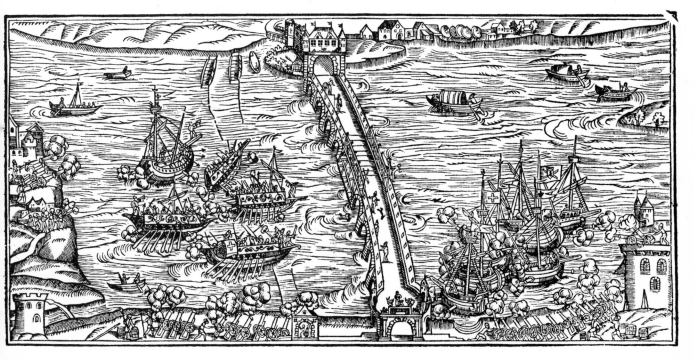

Marie de' Medici's Entry
into Avignon, 1600 (92–3):
92 Henry IV as
Apollo Economo bearing
up the world

prophecies of theologians, astrologers and pamphleteers around the year
1600, the festivals to celebrate the marriage in Florence sing of Henry as
a hero whose military prowess will bring empire and who will lead a new
crusade and free the Holy Sepulchre from the Infidel. In the solemn entries
made by Henry's bride into Avignon and Lyon the King, under the image
of the heroic Gallic Hercules, is cast as a protector of the Faith whose mission of universal pacification augurs imperial power. The programme by
the Jesuit André Valladier, the *Labyrinth royale de l'Hercule Gaulois triom-*
phant,★ for the Avignon entry includes an arch dedicated to Henry as Apollo
Economo, the god who *'gouverne tout l'Univers par ses rayons et occultes*
influences',† and in which the King appeared bearing up the celestial

92

★ 'Royal labyrinth of the triumphant Gallic Hercules.'
† '… governs the whole Universe by his rays and occult influences.'

93

sphere, with, below, Latin inscriptions heroically echoing the imperial Virgilian prophecy of the *Fourth Eclogue* of the ruler who will restore the reign of Saturn, the Age of Gold. In another arch the columns of Hercules bore up a papal tiara and the French crown supported by a sword and a sceptre respectively, with Henry's motto *Duo protegit unus* above, to show, explains Valladier, that by his authority he not only governs his kingdoms but wields his sword in protection of the Church. In this way the humanist dreamland of *renovatio* embodied in the Messianic literature and imagery surrounding Henry of Navarre becomes gradually transmuted into the creation of absolutist monarchy. It is a line of descent that leads directly from the Emperor Charles V to *le Roi Soleil*.

93 *The Columns of Hercules*

94 *Henry II wounded at a tournament, 1559*

4 'Politique' Magnificence
CATHERINE DE'MEDICI

Some five months after the Ship of State rode through the streets of Brussels signalling the end of the age of Charles V, French, Spanish and English deputies assembled at a small French town called Câteau-Cambrésis to negotiate a treaty. In this settlement France finally abandoned her ambitions within the Italian peninsula, only to be compensated by the acquisition of Calais from the English. The peace, as was customary, was sealed by dynastic alliances. Two French princesses were to be married, one to the Duke of Savoy, the other to Philip II of Spain. Exhausted by a disastrous war, from now on the French Crown had to concern itself with internal problems too long delayed and, in particular, with the spread of Calvinism, which had gained converts among a substantial section of the population, including members of the aristocracy. But before the full import of these issues was realized, the marriages were celebrated with elaborate splendour in Paris. One of the fêtes to mark the event was a great tournament in which the King, Henry II, tilted against his captain of the guard. The result was a famous, fatal accident, for the captain's lance pierced the King's helmet and within a matter of days Henry was dead and a child of thirteen ascended the French throne as Francis II.

94

95

95 After Clouet,
Catherine de'Medici

This unexpected event was watched by the Queen, Catherine de'Medici, whose grief was such that she never wore other than mourning for the rest of her life. As a consequence of this dramatic death, this intensely cultivated and artistic Princess suddenly found herself pushed to the centre of the stage. The history of festivals at the Valois court in the second half of the sixteenth century is so closely bound up with her that they can almost be written in biographical terms. For Catherine de'Medici court fêtes were an integral part of her political policy. These costly and magnificent spectacles were designed to demonstrate to foreigners, as Brantôme records, that the country was not *'si totalement ruinée et pauvre, à cause des guerres passées, comme il s'estimoit'*.★ Catherine was the moving spirit behind such occasions and the fête she gave was always acclaimed to be the one most brilliant and original. It gave her pleasure, Brantôme recounts, to present such spectacles, saying that she wished to imitate the ancient Romans in giving her people entertainments, thus averting their more mischievous activities. Alas, for Catherine this policy was a delusion, but for over twenty years the periodic alignment of Catholics and Protestants

★ '… as utterly ruined and poor owing to the recent wars as was generally thought'.

RIGHT 97 *The Valois Tapestries.
Unidentified Barriers. Francis,
Duke of Anjou stands to the right*

in chivalrous fêtes, whose theme was ever that of loyalty to the French Crown and the blessings of peace, was to be one of her major preoccupations.

The political situation she inherited in 1559 was a recurring one and provides the backcloth against which her court festivals or 'magnificences', as they were called, were acted out. In the main at the opening of the 1560s there were three political alignments within France. The first group, in general Catholic, found its leaders among the powerful house of Lorraine, the Guise. The second, mainly of Protestant or Huguenot persuasion, was led by representatives of the Bourbon or Châtillon families. In the middle stood the Crown, bankrupt and with a young, inexperienced King, not strong enough either to dominate or to stand aside from the main, rival, politico-religious groups. As a result, for thirty years the monarchy became dangerously isolated until, in the person of Henry of Navarre, it identified itself decisively with one side. Catherine's own constant support came from her secretaries of state, who dealt with her correspondence, undertook endless negotiations between rival parties, seconded her tireless efforts to achieve peace and, when this was accomplished, helped her to organize the festivals in celebration. Her policy is epitomized in her personal *impresa*, a rainbow with a motto in Greek meaning: 'It brings peace and serenity'. The difficulty she contended with

96

96 *Rainbow 'impresa' of
Catherine de' Medici*

RIGHT VIII *The Valois
Tapestries. Court ball
following the 'Ballet of the
Provinces of France', 1573*

was that one religious war always tended to lead to the next, that each side
perpetually claimed to act in self-defence, and that the mutual fear this
engendered resulted in a total breakdown of confidence between all the
parties concerned. In the middle Catherine laboured away, faced with a
bankrupt exchequer, a corrupt and unreformed Church, fearing the
growing might of Spain on both borders, and coping with the problem of
how to allow a religious minority to practise its faith without being
molested. Her policy was always one of peace and moderation – later
embodied in the expression *'politique'* – and finds vivid artistic expression
in her court festivals. Once, in 1572, in the midst of such a set of conciliatory fêtes, through panic, it broke down and the result was the Massacre
of St Bartholomew. The terrible *'noces vermeilles'**★* of Marguerite de Valois
and Henry of Navarre have obscured the central theme of Catherine's life
and made her lose her place as a creative genius in the art of the festival.

The fêtes of the last Valois are marvellously evoked in two sets of visual
documents. The most famous is the set of eight tapestries known as the
Valois Tapestries, now in the Uffizi in Florence, probably by way of
Catherine's adopted daughter and heir, Christina of Lorraine, Grand
Duchess of Florence. The second is a series of drawings by Antoine Caron,
five in number, which survive and are now scattered in various collections.
These are related in subject matter to the tapestries and were obviously
connected with their manufacture, but are not always identical in content.
Together with a handful of illustrated books, these convey a very vivid
and coherent picture of the aesthetic style and artistic magnificence of
Valois festival art. Certain of the tapestries and drawings depict readily

*Plate IX
97*

identifiable occasions – the water fête at Bayonne or the ballet for the
Polish ambassadors. Others, such as the attack on an elephant, or the barriers, remain unidentified and mysterious. Identification is not helped by
the unevennness of written evidence or by artistic licence, which sometimes turns an indoor entertainment into an alfresco one, besides inserting
into the foreground, in the case of the tapestries, a series of portrait figures
of the royal family at a later date than the occasion enacted behind them.
Both tapestries and drawings were done in retrospect, but the latter
definitely precede the former in date and therefore probably give a more
accurate impression of the visual appearance of Catherine's 'magnificences'. The author of the drawings, moreover, was a favourite of the

OVERLEAF 98 Antoine
Caron, *Festival for the
Polish Ambassadors, 1573.
Catherine de' Medici's
entertainment*

★ 'Bloody nuptials.'

OPPOSITE IX *The Valois
Tapestries. Unidentified
festival. An assault upon
an elephant*

Queen Mother's and of the humanists who devised the fêtes. Caron collaborated with them in producing décor for entries and 'magnificences' over the years. The latest certain identifiable event in both drawings and tapestries dates to 1573, and the gentle sloping silhouette of female costume is not later than about 1580. Both must also have had access to lost manuscript sources to achieve such archaeologically correct reconstructions.

The Valois court fêtes, unlike those of Charles V, are also significant for being animated by a single artistic policy, that of the revival of 'ancient music' and 'ancient poetry'. Ronsard praised Mellin de Saint-Gelais for being the first French poet to marry poetry and music in the ancient Greek way, a movement which was to find concrete form in Jean-Antoine de Baïf's establishment of the Académie de Poésie et de Musique in 1570. The aims of the Academy were the union of music and verse as it had been in antiquity, and through this union the revival of the ethical effects of ancient music on the listener. Such a renewal of ancient metric modes, epitomized in *musique mesurée*, was believed to have enormous 'effects' on the audience. The most famous story of the success that this movement achieved occurred at just such a set of 'magnificences', those staged to mark the marriage of Henry III's favourite, the Duke of Joyeuse, in 1581. During a foot-combat a warlike Phrygian song caused one gentleman present to rise from his seat and begin to draw his sword for the fight, his martial ardour being forthwith soothed to calm by a sub-Phrygian air. This union of music and poetry also included attempts to re-create 'ancient dancing', based on the rhythmic principles of *musique mesurée*. The Academy arranged practical experiments of dances executed to *chanson mesurée*, thus unifying poetry, music and the dance. Choreographed dances were always Catherine de'Medici's especial contribution to any set of 'magnificences' and her preoccupation with choreography, together with the humanist aims of the Academy, led to the birth of a new art form, the celebrated French *ballet de cour*. The actual history of the Academy is obscure, but in 1577 either a replacement or an extension of it was founded, the Académie du Palais. Much concerned with philosophical debates and with aspects of Henry III's religious exercises, it still continued the traditions of musical humanism embodied in the original foundation. The festivals of Catherine de'Medici were always therefore influenced more or less directly by the programme represented in this academic movement.

99 *The Valois Tapestries. Catherine de' Medici*

Catherine summed up her own position admirably in a letter to her daughter Elizabeth: 'God ... has left me with three small children, and in a kingdom utterly divided, in which there is not a soul in whom I can trust at all, who has not got some private purpose of his own.' Her eldest son Francis II died in 1560, and Catherine assumed the reins of government on behalf of the new King, Charles IX, then aged ten, with Anthony, King of Navarre, whom she could control, as Lieutenant-General of the kingdom. Catherine's hopes for a solution to the religious divisions separating the realm centred on the summoning of a new General Council at which the Protestants would be heard. Failing this, she threatened to summon a National Council of the Gallican Church which would reform its own house in defiance of Rome. All the Queen Mother ultimately obtained was a new session of the Council of Trent, where the liberal demands made by the French delegation were promptly rejected. In reply Catherine held a colloquy at Poissy attended by theologians of the two creeds, a meeting which ended in total failure. While these royal efforts at conciliation were happening, however, the rival parties had already coalesced: the Duke of Guise, the Constable Montmorency and the Maréchal de St-André in the Catholic interest, and the King of Navarre together with the Prince de Condé in the Huguenot. In January 1562 Catherine took matters into her own hands and issued an Edict of Toleration granting the Protestants certain rights to practise their faith. Three months later the soldiers of the Duke of Guise massacred some Protestants worshipping in a barn, an event which precipitated the first religious war. This came to an end the year after, fortunately for Catherine removing most of the troublemakers: Navarre was killed at the siege of Rouen, the Maréchal de St-André fell at the battle of Dreux and the Duke of Guise was assassinated. In March 1563 Catherine celebrated the re-establishment of peace with the first set of her 'magnificences' at Chenonceaux. Little is known about them, but they included a firework display, a water fête, a picnic and a masque. We know only details concerning the fête on arrival, when the royal party advanced up the tree-lined avenue to be met by singing sirens who were answered by nymphs from the nearby wood. Satyrs entered and attempted to carry off the nymphs but they were rescued by knights. These singing sirens were to be a standard ingredient of the mythology of every set of 'magnificences' for the next twenty years.

Chenonceaux reads like a dress rehearsal for Catherine's next set of conciliatory 'magnificences', which took place at Fontainebleau at the beginning of 1564. Here the court had assembled prior to the *Grand Voyage de France* to receive ambassadors from the Pope and the Catholic princes come to ask that the French King publish the decrees of the Council of Trent within his domains and unite in a campaign to exterminate heresy. The requests were swiftly declined as being contrary to the liberties of the Gallican Church and it was in an atmosphere of the rejection of Tridentine Catholicism and of religious conciliation that the first set of 'magnificences' were staged. They also reflected Catherine's wish to create a brilliant court centring round her son. In Brantôme's words she made it *'un vray Paradis du monde'*.

The fêtes were given by various people. There was a combat on horseback presented by the Cardinal of Bourbon, a banquet and a comedy by the Duchess of Angoulême, a barriers by the Duke of Orléans and the storming of a castle by the King. One of these combats was between Greek and Trojan knights on the theme of love. The knights carried shields with devices painted upon them and the heroic deeds of each combatant were recited to music by heralds. The King's festival was modelled on that of the famous *Château Ténébreux* at Binche in 1549, and the elaborate décor included a castle guarded by a giant, in which certain ladies were held prisoner by a magician, and a hermitage from which the knights made their entrance to fight. Ultimately the spell was broken, inevitably by the King, accompanied by his brother, Anjou. Catherine's own entertainment took place on the canal at Fontainebleau one morning, when the King was met by three sirens who sang loyal songs, with verses by Ronsard, casting the reign within a pastoral milieu. They tell how the reign of Henry II had been a Golden Age which now his son, the shepherd Carlin, Charles IX, is about to revive, having already chased away the phantom of war which had caused the gentle deities of sea and land to hide themselves. Now they reappear to celebrate the glory of the French monarchy. Later Neptune rode along the canal in a sea chariot drawn by four sea horses and a nymph appeared on a rock.

The Fontainebleau 'magnificences' formed the pattern for those to come. They were always to consist of a series of fêtes spread over a number of days with intervals in between and various people giving the entertainments on the different days. By 1572, if not earlier, this included the whole court wearing a particular colour for each event as it happened. In general each set of 'magnificences' had two types of spectacle. The first was predominantly chivalrous. This included a barriers, running at the quintain, a tourney between two groups of knights or the storming of a fortress. As the reign progressed this was increasingly diversified with music and song within a framework of dramatic action. Under the influence of Catherine these martial sports were tamed and their importance was gradually lessened by her own contributions. These made up the second type of spectacle and took a rather hybrid form, making use of pageant cars, water, feasting, singing and dancing but knitted together to create something original. Brantôme records that the Queen Mother could always be relied upon to produce some new and beautiful experience. In the early stages the form was loose and processional but as the reign progressed it tautened. Out of it emerged that most distinctive form of French festival art, the celebrated *ballet de cour*.

At the close of the Fontainebleau 'magnificences' the court left on a two-year ceremonial progress through the provinces of France so that the young King could be displayed to his subjects and thus support could be engendered for the Crown. Throughout the tour the Edict of Pacification was rigorously enforced. Each town received the King with a solemn entry in the manner accorded to his predecessors. Contemporary accounts dwell on the poverty of these occasions, reflecting as they did a kingdom wasted through civil war and disturbance. The author of the account of the King's entry into Rouen the year before, in August 1563, remembers the glory of former occasions and reflects sadly on present poverty, on how not even enough tailors remained to make the costumes for the customary formal procession with which the entry had opened. That at Lyon in June 1564 was recorded as being *'ny sumptueuse en habits, ny ingenieuse en apparat de Theatres & Perspectives'.*★ The ravages of war were everywhere vividly recalled. At Lyon, Discord was chained and the entry included the remarkable sight of Catholic and Protestant children walking together in procession. Apollo and the Muses optimistically sang of a new Golden Age:

> *O Charles de Valoys,*
> *Mon Prince, o Siècle d'Or, tu sois le bien venu.*★

The furthest point the court reached on its progress was the Spanish frontier, where from 15 June to 2 July 1565 took place the famous encounter of the French and Spanish courts known as the Bayonne Interview. Politically the occasion was a disaster. Catherine had hoped that Philip II would come in person so that she could explain her religious policy. In the end Philip sent his wife, Catherine's daughter, Elizabeth, and, as his own representative, the Duke of Alva. They carried strict instructions to offer an alliance only to exterminate heresy, with further demands that Huguenot ministers should be banished, that Huguenots should be deprived of office, and that Catherine should see that the decrees of the Council of Trent were put into effect within her kingdom. Catherine's optimistic belief that personal contact would enable her to persuade her son-in-law to reopen the question of a new General Council of the Church and of an agreement on further Valois and Habsburg marriages was met with a rude rebuttal.

The fêtes, therefore, celebrated a non-existent Hispano-French *entente*. On one day there was running at the ring in fancy dress, on another an enchanted castle was stormed and taken by Charles IX; there was a tourney *Plate VIII* between the Knights of Great Britain and Ireland, and finally Catherine's own entertainment, an elaborate water festival that included a voyage, a banquet and a ballet. The tourney took place on 25 June and consisted of eight knights on either side defending Love and Virtue respectively. The cartels were sung to the lyre and each side was preceded into the arena by a chariot. The British Knights had Heroic Virtue and four other Virtues

---

★ '... neither sumptuous in dress, nor ingenious in its theatrical and perspective displays.'

★ 'Oh, Charles of Valois,/My Prince, Oh Golden Age, thou art welcome.'

100 Antoine Caron, *Festival at Bayonne, 1565.*
Tourney of the Knights of Great Britain and Ireland

with the nine Muses, and the Irish carried Venus, the three Graces and nine
little Loves or Passions. The Muses and Passions mounted the tilt gallery,
101 in which the ladies sat, and gave them jewels bearing the devices painted
102 on the knights' shields. The official *Recueil* of these events contains engravings of them and a number can be identified in the Valois Tapestry
that depicts the occasion. Both the Caron drawing and the tapestry represent the final phase of the entertainment, the general mêlée, when fireballs
100 were tossed between the horses, which pranced to and fro with a dexterity
that was the cause for much admiration.

Catherine's water festival was the last of the series. The anonymous
103 author of the *Recueil* begins by a frank explanation of the Queen Mother's
aims. He writes that she wished through this meeting to secure not only
peace and the union of the two kingdoms, but through this *'le bien
vniversal de toute la Chrestienté'.*★ Embarking on a boat constructed like a
castle the royal party sailed through a series of canals to an island upon
which Catherine had constructed an octagonal banqueting house. As they

★ 'The universal well-being of Christendom.'

134

103 *The Valois Tapestries. Festival at Bayonne, 1565.*
Catherine de'Medici's water fête

LEFT ABOVE 101 *Pendant device of*
Charles IX
LEFT BELOW 102 *Pendant device of*
Henry III as Duke of Anjou

TOP 103a *The attack on the whale*
CENTRE LEFT b *Tritons riding on a tortoise*
CENTRE MIDDLE c *Neptune*
CENTRE RIGHT d *Arion*
BELOW LEFT e *The Sirens*
BELOW RIGHT f *The dance of the Shepherds*

103a
103b
103c
journeyed they passed various scenes: firstly, there was an attack on a whale led by men in boats which lasted half an hour; secondly, a marine tortoise appeared, upon which sat six musicians as tritons, who struck up music at the sight of Charles IX; thirdly, there was Neptune in a car drawn by sea-horses. Both the Valois Tapestry and Caron's drawing show these incidents in detail and up until now all had been in the vein of the Fontainebleau festivals of the previous year. Neptune was followed by
103d
103e
Arion on a dolphin's back and three sirens, who combined in loyal songs, saying that now the time was propitious to greet Charles and his sister, the Queen of Spain. On landing there were dances by shepherds and shepherdesses, after which the party proceeded up a *grande allée* to be met by Orpheus and Linus together with three nymphs, who sang songs with verses that sum up the whole theme of the day's spectacle:

> *ie voy le François & L'Ibère*
> *Ioincts & unis, non point comme estrangiers,*
> *Mais tout ainsi que deux freres Bergiers.*
> *Tant que viura Philippe & Ysabeau,*
> *Tant que viura Charles & Catherine,*
> *Ny l'Espagnol ny le François troupeau*
> *Craindra le Nord sa froide bruine:*
> *Tant que seront quatre d'vn accord,*
> *Entre Bergiers il n'y aura discord.*★

103f
The peace of France and Spain is celebrated in the terms of idyllic Golden Age pastoral life. After a banquet had been served by the shepherds and shepherdesses six violinists entered and struck up the music for nine nymphs who danced a ballet, after which the royal party returned as they had come.

104
Both the Caron drawings and the Valois Tapestries evoke these splendid festivals with considerable accuracy, although there are variations in costume and architectural detail. In both the chariots of Love and Virtue can be seen standing on either side of the tilt gallery, while the Muses and the nine little Passions present their jewelled medallions to the chosen ladies. In the middle distance the rival groups of British and Irish Knights, led by

---

★ '... behold the Frenchman and the Spaniard/Joined and united, not like strangers/But just like a pair of shepherd Brothers./As long as Philip and Elizabeth/As long as Charles and Catherine shall live,/Neither the Spanish nor the French flock/shall fear the North or its chilly drizzle:/As long as all four are of one accord/Beween Shepherds there shall be no discord.'

137

the King and his brother Anjou respectively, engage in the general mêlée. The Caron drawing for the water festival gives a much clearer idea of the sequence of dramatic experience by the voyagers, while the tapestry includes striking first-hand details such as the *grande allée* and, above all, the fact that the shepherds and shepherdesses wore regional French costumes for their dances, while the royal party disembarked and made its way towards the avenue. Catherine's brilliant but difficult daughter Marguerite de Valois, who stands in the front of the event to the left with her husband Henry of Navarre, provides this fact in her memoirs and further describes the scene:

These shepherdesses, during the passage of the superb boats from Bayonne to the island, were placed in separate bands, in a meadow on each side of the causeway, raised with turf. ... After landing, the shepherdesses I have mentioned before received the company in separate troops, with sinop and dances, after the fashion and accompanied by the music of the provinces they represented – the Poiterins playing on bagpipes; the Provençales on the viol and cymbal; the Burgundians and Champagners on the hautboy, bass viol, and tambourine; in like manner the Bretons and other provincialists. After the collation was served and the feast at an end, a large troop of musicians, habited like satyrs, were seen to come out of the opening of a rock, well lighted up, whilst nymphs were descending from the top in rich habits, who, as they came down, formed into a grand dance. ...

The component parts of the fêtes are an elaboration on Fontainebleau. The whale on the journey symbolized war vanquished before the eyes of the onlooking voyagers – internal civil war and war between Habsburg and Valois – the monster once subdued, it became possible for the shy sea and land deities once more, as at Fontainebleau, to make their presence felt. Harmony is taken from water to land by the shepherdesses in their dances. This theme of innocent country pastimes restored in time of peace was repeated again and again during the *Grand Voyage de France*, for whatever region the King visited the local dances always formed a part of the entertainment. Such a cultivation of peasant pleasures as symbolic of peaceful good government can be paralleled as much in the peasant *kermesse* paintings of Breughel as in the progress entertainments of Elizabeth I. In contrast to Fontainebleau there is a shift in dramatic emphasis, the main part of the entertainment being the dance. Out of these dances performed in a field by the shepherdess in regional costume, and out of the ballet by nymphs at the close, developed the French *ballet de cour*.

104 Antoine Caron, *Festival at Bayonne 1565.*
Catherine de' Medici's water fête

The dance forms such an important part in the story of Valois court festival that it is necessary to pause in our narrative and ask why more and more it began to occupy a significant place in the make-up of late sixteenth- and particularly seventeenth-century court fêtes. To the Renaissance mind the dance essentially represented harmony in its capacity as a reflection of heavenly order. It was held that the dance arose through an imitation of the movements of the stars and planets. Thoinot Arbeau advises the reader in his *Orchesography*, published in 1588, to practise the dances he describes carefully that he may 'become a fit companion of the planets, who dance of their own nature'. Sir John Davies, celebrating Elizabeth I, describes the dance of the elements in creating the measured order of the cosmos:

> Dauncing (bright Lady) then began to be,
> When the first seedes whereof the world did spring,
> The Fire, Ayre, Earth, and water did agree,
> By Loues perswasion, Natures mighty King,
> To leaue their first disordred combating;
> > And in daunce such measure to observe,
> > As all the world their motion should preserue.

For Renaissance theorists the dance was a moral exercise affording virtuous contemplation and giving pleasure to the intellect. The passionate Renaissance belief in correspondences between the celestial and the sublunar worlds gave dancing and music, to which it was allied, a place of tremendous importance in attempts to relate the one to the other. The power of movement, itself a reflection of the action of the spheres, was intensified by its union with music, similarly a terrestrial manifestation of a celestial phenomenon, the music of the spheres. Bayonne may seem a very far cry from this theorizing, but by the opening of the next century the dance was to become one of the most perfect visual vehicles through which to express theories of absolute monarchy. As we follow the development of the use of dance in Valois court festivals, it gradually becomes a way to express a political order of things. By bringing spectators into the chain by the introduction of general dancing after the main ballet, it became the ideal vehicle, in both France and England, for drawing the onlookers into the ideological theme of the spectacle. In this audience participation they 'renewed' themselves and outwardly demonstrated their adherence to the ideal principles of government expounded in the court fête. This was incipient at Bayonne, but it was to be taken a decisive stage further seven years later in the next great series of 'magnificences', those to mark the Protestant-Catholic marriage of Henry of Navarre to Marguerite de Valois.

During the intervening years war broke out again twice, once in 1567, ending in the Treaty of Longjumeau the year after, only to break out again, this time ending in August 1570 with the Treaty of Saint-Germain. Both treaties ratified the enforcement of the Edict of Pacification and the latter went dangerously further by granting the Huguenots certain *places de sûreté* for their faith. Catherine's policy during this period centred heavily on matches for her children: Anjou and subsequently Alençon to Elizabeth I; Marguerite to Henry of Navarre and Charles IX to Elizabeth of Austria, daughter of the Emperor Maximilian II. Through these matches a pattern of conciliatory alliances would be formed throughout Europe, and this was to be complemented by concerted efforts against Spanish oppression in the Low Countries. In July 1570 William of Orange's brother, Louis of Nassau, asked Charles IX and Catherine for a French army to liberate the Low Countries. This activity in relation to the Netherlands led to a *rapprochement* with the new leader of the Huguenots, Admiral Coligny, who began to have an increasing influence over the King that Catherine was later to regret. During these years a pattern of anti-Spanish alliances was formed. On 11 April 1572 the contract of marriage between Henry of Navarre and Marguerite de Valois was sealed. Eight days later a treaty of peace was signed with England and marriage negotiations with Elizabeth began in earnest. Magnificent embassies were exchanged and splendid fêtes were given on both sides of the Channel. In England the occasion was marked by a brilliant midnight tourney at Whitehall with speeches in French on the theme of Peace, who arrived in a chariot, seeking succour at the English court.

The most documented festival event of these years, however, was the entry made into Paris by Charles IX and his Queen, Elizabeth of Austria, in March 1571. On this event Pierre Ronsard and Jean Dorat collaborated with Germain Pilon, the sculptor, and Niccolò dell'Abbate, the painter. The themes were resonant of the entry of Charles's father, Henry II, over twenty years earlier, using recurrent motifs – the antiquity of the French royal house, represented by the Trojans Francus and Pharamond, the usual

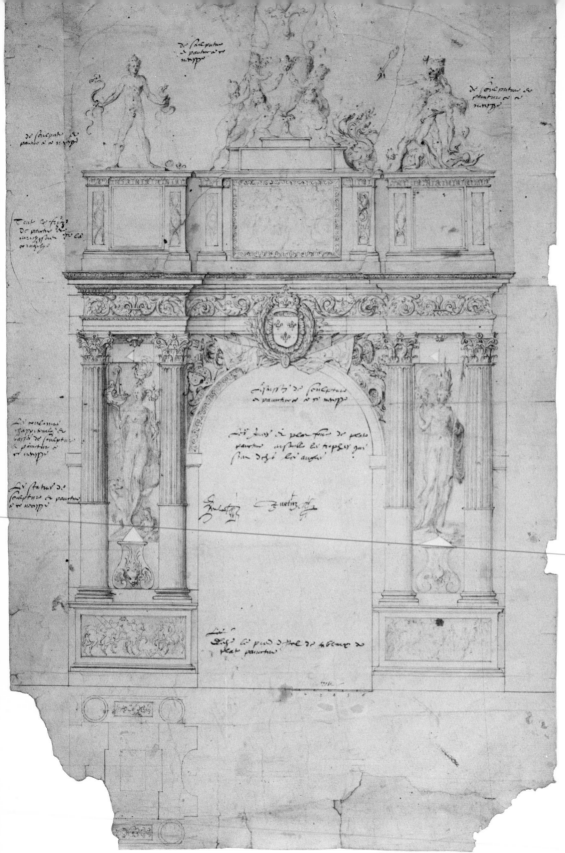

*Entries of Charles IX and
Elizabeth of Austria into
Paris, 1571 (105–8):
105 Entry of Charles IX.
Design by Giulio Camillo
Abate for the arch at the
Porte aux Peintres*

arch dedicated to the city with the ship of France flanked by Castor and Pollux, the two stars promising good fortune at sea, and the obligatory humanist casting of the French royal family as a new Olympus. The entry was heavy with Renaissance hieroglyphics and reveals the erudite classicism demanded by the city governors. To take a single instance, the figure of Paris on the arch dedicated to the three royal brothers: Paris bore the *fasces* and the ship, emblem of the city; she was also accompanied by a golden fleece, signifying commerce, books, alluding to the arts and sciences, a cock, referring to the wisdom and vigilance of her governors, and a dog, representing the humility with which she offered herself to the King. The themes as a whole were those of peace and empire, both made richer and fuller by this union of a King of France with a daughter of sacred empire.

Elizabeth herself was ill when the entry took place, so much was the consternation of the city fathers when a second entry was asked for, which took place three weeks later. Great was the panic and confusion of poets and artists. The demolition of the existing decorations was stopped and their adaptation put in hand with all possible speed. Francus and Pharamond became Charlemagne; Hymen, god of marriage, became Saturn; and Castor and Pollux were replaced by Europa and the Bull. The marriage of the two Troy-descended monarchs presaged this time not only the union of Europe but a child who would conquer the Orient and rule the world. The nymph on the bull was not Europa but Asia, and the *Recueil*

LEFT 106 *Entry of Charles IX. Arch with the Ship of Paris flanked by Castor and Pollux*
RIGHT 107 *Entry of Elizabeth. Arch with the nymph Asia and the bull*

143

recounts that it meant that the Dauphin *'ravira l'Asie et le reste du monde, pour joindre à son empire et soy faire monarque de l'Univers'*.★ But the Queen's entry had an artistic significance in the banquet accorded to the King and Queen after the entry in a room decorated with twenty-four canvases by Niccolò dell'Abbate after an extraordinarily recondite programme devised by Jean Dorat. These illustrated the story of Bacchus' son, Cadmus of Thebes, as told by the fifth-century Greek poet, Nonnos of Panopolis. Its climax was the central ceiling panel, in which Cadmus and his bride, Harmony, rode in a great ship with four other smaller ships, representing Religion, Justice, Nobility and Merchandise, chained to it. In other words the vision was of the royal couple guiding the ship of France, also an emblem of the city of Paris, with the four Estates of the realm, to a happy haven of peace and imperial greatness.

★ '… will violate Asia and the rest of the world, so as to add them to his empire and make himself monarch of the Universe.'

108 *Triumphal car, with Charles IX's column 'impresa', presented to the King by the City of Paris on the occasion of the Queen's Entry*

109 Antoine Caron, *Unidentified 'course'*
in fancy dress

OVERLEAF X *The Valois Tapestries.*
Tourney of the Knights of Great
Britain and Ireland, Bayonne, 1565

145

110 *The Valois Tapestries. Unidentified*
'course' in fancy dress. Henry III, in
antique costume, mounts his horse to the right

The 'magnificences' for the Navarre-Valois wedding the year after were planned as a series in the same way as their predecessors. No one attending the opening fêtes could have had any premonition that this gathering of Catholic and Protestant leaders in fraternal rejoicings to celebrate a marriage that epitomized the culmination of the policy of conciliation would end in the bloody Massacre of St Bartholomew. When they began on 17 August with the customary *fiançailles* everything was set for the usual mixture of chivalrous combats, masquerades and allegorical shows in which members of rival religious creeds united to honour the Crown and pay tribute to the new bride and groom. After the marriage, on the Monday, there was a masquerade in which the King, the Protestants Navarre and Condé and the ultra-Catholic Duke of Guise entered the hall on marine chariots encrusted with coral and sea-creatures. Charles IX played Neptune and the deities descended from their mobile sea-grottoes and danced. This was the mythology of the Fontainebleau and Bayonne fêtes brought indoors. On Tuesday there was a court ball at the Louvre, while on Wednesday there followed an allegorical combat in the Salle de Bourbon of the Louvre, entitled *Le Paradis d'Amour*. This was the most spectacular of all the entertainments that actually took place. Surviving accounts prove that others were planned but never executed because of the disastrous interruption to the festivities.

Le Paradis d'Amour was a development from the enchanted castle combats of the earlier fêtes, but this time with a climax in the dance. From what little we know of it, *Le Paradis d'Amour* is also a crucial moment in the development of the new art of *ballet de cour*. The décor was of the usual scattered variety. Charles IX and his two brothers, Anjou and Alençon, defended the gateway to Paradise, behind which stretched the Elysian Fields, in which there resided twelve nymphs and in which revolved a huge model of the heavens. To the left there was the Underworld, with a hell mouth approached by crossing a river in a boat manned by Charon. Into the room came troops of knights in different liveries who fought at the barriers and, as they were defeated by the brothers, were relegated to the Underworld. In this almost theological setting the attackers were ominously led by Henry of Navarre, a fact regarded in retrospect as especially sinister and prophetic of future happenings. But there was nothing unusual in the pattern of the plot, for the royal brothers always had to win, as they had in previous fancy-dress tournaments. This time, however, the dramatic sequence was changed. After the fighting, instead of the usual celebrations with fireworks to mark the victory of the royal family, Etienne Le Roy, the famous singer, descended from the heavens as Mercury accompanied by Cupid and harangued the royal brothers on the virtues of love. They subsequently led out the twelve nymphs from the Elysian Fields and danced a complicated ballet that lasted for an hour. This brought to its conclusion, the imprisoned knights were released from the Underworld, conceivably at the intercession of the nymphs, in allusion to the pacifying power of love instanced in the Navarre-Valois wedding. The entertainment was brought to its close with the customary fireworks. In its mixture of dramatic plot, scenery, singing and dancing it is well on the way to the new form of *ballet de cour*.

On Thursday, 21 August there was a *course de bague* in the courtyard of the Louvre. Charles IX and his brothers appeared as Amazons, the Prince de Condé *à l'estradiotte* and the Duke of Guise as another Amazon. The event must have looked very like the unidentified *course* in the Caron drawing, which takes place in a courtyard with architecture directly of the Louvre type. Ladies lean down from the tilt gallery in the background, trumpeters sound from the colonnade to the left, while a knight in fancy dress runs his course. In the Valois Tapestry this event is transferred into the open and Henry III in Roman costume is placed before it. To the left, however, can be seen a group of masked knights dressed as Amazons with trailing skirts falling over their horses, awaiting their turn at the running. In the distance sits Catherine, a dark figure in mourning, as always presiding over the occasion.

On 22 August, the day after, between ten and eleven o'clock in the morning, Admiral Coligny was shot at and wounded from a house, soon after discovered to be one belonging to the Duke of Guise. The panic this produced precipitated the series of events leading to the order for the Massacre. Contrary to most of what the policy of Catherine de' Medici had ever stood for, and contrary to the spirit of the Navarre-Valois marriage, the bloody Massacre burst on to the scene. Its horrors were immediately perpetrated through the rest of France, leading to a resumption of civil war. Strangely enough it made virtually no difference whatever to royal policy. As quickly as possible it was realized that this had been the most ghastly mistake. Catherine renewed her relations with William of Orange and Louis of Nassau against Spain in the Low Countries, and once more refused to publish the decrees of the Council of Trent. From one

109

110

point of view the Massacre was an insane blunder, for it occurred at the very moment when Catherine was projecting the most liberal and tolerant policy possible in order that her favourite son, Anjou, should be elected King of Poland.

On 7 July 1572, a month before the Navarre-Valois 'magnificences', Sigismund II of Poland died and the Polish Diet met to elect a new king. Poland was unique in Europe in the sixteenth century for being the only country where liberty of conscience was an established fact. It was, therefore, with great difficulty that Catherine's most conciliatory envoy, Jean Monluc, Bishop of Valence, explained away the Massacre. On 9 May 1573 the Polish Diet actually elected Anjou king, but only on condition that he maintained liberty of conscience. Two months later, on 6 July, Charles IX issued the Edict of Boulogne, bringing an end to the war provoked by the Massacre and establishing once more liberty of conscience within France. In this way, less than a year after, Catherine was back where she had started. In the light of a crown for Anjou, everything was to be stage-managed as though the Massacre had never happened.

One year later, almost to the day, the Polish ambassadors made their entry into Paris. The impression they made in their magnificent costumes, recorded in the Caron drawing and the Valois Tapestry, was one of barbaric richness and splendour. There seems to have been the usual set of 'magnificences', preceded by Anjou's entry into Paris as King of Poland. This was devised by Jean Dorat and it presented the happy, if totally untrue, picture of the three united brothers, the grief of France at the loss of Anjou, and the heroism of the Queen Mother, depicted as Pallas, hymned as the mother of kings and bringer of peace. There was even an allusion on one arch to that other match which animated her policy of conciliation, that of her most troublesome son, Alençon, with Elizabeth I of England. But the greatest spectacle was the ballet staged by the Queen Mother herself in the gardens of the Tuileries. Sixteen ladies of the court, including her daughter Marguerite de Valois, then at her most sparkling, were revealed seated on a silver rock attired as the provinces of France. To the most melodious music that had ever been heard, it is recorded, they toured a hall ablaze with flambeaux. The ladies afterwards descended from the rock and danced a spectacular ballet, which lasted for an hour. Not a step was out of place and their intricate movement and patterns, together with their grace, made a profound effect on the audience.

98
Plate X

111

112

Rock bearing the dancers in the 'Ballet of the Provinces of France', 1573

Nothing quite like it in the way of sustained choreography had ever been seen before. Brantôme records that it was *'le plus beau ballet qui fut jamais fait au monde'*★ and the Poles said that *'le bal de France estoit chose impossible à contrefaire à tous les rois de la terre'.*†

Agrippa d'Aubigny records that the court ball that followed continued for most of the night. The feeble woodcut illustrating the official account, Dorat's *Magnificentissimi Spectaculi*, shows something of the appearance of the temporary *salle des fêtes* and, above all, the court ladies arranged in a figure. This is the earliest representation of a choreographed ballet. In both the Caron drawing and the tapestry the walls of the hall are taken away and we are shown the court ball in action. In the foreground are the Poles

112

Plate X
98

★ '... the most beautiful ballet the world has ever known.'
† '... the French dance could not possibly be imitated by any king on earth.'

in their national dress, while in the background stretch the gardens of the Tuileries. From these sources we learn that the musicians on that occasion were dressed as Apollo and the Muses and also sat upon a rock. *The Ballet of the Provinces of France* included the presentation of symbolic devices, an element from the Bayonne tournament of the Knights of Great Britain and Ireland. Its mythology re-echoed the county dances in provincial costume at Bayonne but in its outstanding development in coherence and in the elaboration of dance it was already a new form of spectacle. And, as in all the greatest festivals, the dominating figure is the Queen Mother who sits looking at her own creation in her flowing widow's weeds.

Almost a decade separates the 'magnificences' for the Polish ambassadors from those for the wedding of Anne, Duke of Joyeuse, in 1581. These were the years of the reign of Catherine's most gifted and most complex son,

113 Artist unknown, *Ball at the court of Henry III.*
Henry III and Catherine de' Medici stand to the left

113

Henry III, who succeeded in 1574. Intellectual and introspective, Henry III was the wrong king to rule over a France divided by religion, ruined by civil war and bankrupt. By far the cleverest of Catherine's sons, he was seized by alternate bouts of feverish activity and total inertia. As the reign progressed the latter tended to predominate. Prone to morbid suspicion of those round him, he was also a hopeless judge of character and incapable of realizing the consequences of his own actions. The reign opened with the united family disintegrating. On 15 September Marguerite and Alençon, who hated his brother, fled from the court. Navarre had already left and now headed the Huguenots. Poor Catherine spent most of her time trying to re-establish concord among her remaining sons and daughter. While the power of the Catholic cause led by the Guise and with support from Spain grew, the Crown was becoming even more dangerously isolated and its position was not helped by the open defiance of Alençon. These were years when Catherine struggled to preserve government from breaking down, tried to stop Alençon intervening in the Low Countries and to arrange a marriage for him with Elizabeth I.

The Joyeuse 'magnificences' celebrated the marriage of Henry III's favourite, Anne, Duke of Joyeuse, to Marguerite, sister of Queen Louise of Lorraine. These 'magnificences' were not the conciliatory fêtes of yore, in which Protestant and Catholic knights joined in peaceful chivalrous combat to demonstrate their allegiance to the Crown. The Joyeuse 'magnificences' exalted a royal favourite almost into a member of the royal family and represented the Crown allying itself closely by marriage to the ultra-Catholic Guise faction. This exaltation alienated the aristocracy and the shocking expenditure of a million *écus* on the wedding fêtes was bitterly denounced in view of the mounting royal debts and the collapse of ordered government in the provinces. The 'magnificences' occurred during an interval of peace, for on 26 November 1580 the Treaty of Fleix was signed. At the opening of 1581 Henry III had a long illness, after which his eccentricity and immoderation became worse. For the marriage the bride's father, Duke Charles of Lorraine, and his court came to Paris and the fêtes were without doubt the climax of Valois festival art. In the dedication of his *Mimes* to Joyeuse, de Baïf wrote that he was still trying to collect his wits after so many '*magnifiques théâtres, spectacles, courses, combats, mascarades, ballets, poësies, peintures*',★ which had been

★ '… magnificent theatres, shows, races, combats, masquerades, ballets, poems, paintings.'

155

specially created in honour of the alliance. Cartels were composed by Ronsard and Desportes, an epithalamion by de Baïf, music by Claude Le Jeune and décor by Antoine Caron. The King paid the contributors handsomely for their labours and in these fêtes more than in any other we are able to trace the fruits of the poetic and musical programme of the Académie de Poésie et de Musique.

As usual the 'magnificences' extended over a fortnight and were given on various days by different people. Each day had its own particular colours: one would be white and silver and another silver and pink. Due to conflicting accounts of the entertainments it is difficult to establish exactly when all the events took place and our knowledge of each one varies greatly. They apparently opened on 19 September with a foot-combat presented by the Duke of Mercoeur in the Salle de Bourbon in the Louvre between the King and the Dukes of Guise, of Mercoeur and of Damville who fought for and against Love. The King's party was against Love, and he and his companions entered on a rock clad in black, carnation and green, Love chained at their feet with musicians attired *à l'antique*, who sang Le Jeune's '*La Guerre*', a song sung with menacing gestures telling of the dolours of love. Other knights who came to defend Love had a cartel by Ronsard, and Desportes wrote another for a troop calling themselves the Faithful Knights. On the wedding day there was apparently a *course de bague* in which the King's troop arrived in white, black and silver, each one preceded by a lance-bearer disguised as a captive king in chains. They were accompanied by six Moors on a camel, who sang '*en langue estrangère*'. This was listed on the programme for the fêtes, although we have no evidence that it was actually executed. An epithalamion by de Baïf, however, was certainly performed on the day of the wedding. Two choirs of boys and girls dressed *à l'antique* led in by Hymen sang verses in hexameters in *vers mesurés* to *musique mesurée* by Le Jeune. There was a tourney at night in the courtyard of the Louvre in which knights fought fourteen a side in white and yellow. For this '*un theatre pompeux, & deux braves arcades*',★ one representing the Moon and the other the Sun, had been constructed. The décor apparently included a gigantic representation of the heavens with the planets moving in their courses and the emblems of the French royal house included, foretelling, surprisingly in the circumstances, the happy destiny of the family. Henry III entered '*comme un grand*

★ '... a ceremonial theatre, & two splendid arcades'.

soleil estival',★ an anticipation of Louis XIV as the Sun King. For another tournament, also in the courtyard of the Louvre, he came in a marine triumph, riding on a great ship floating in a sea full of rocks with musicians dressed as tritons. These sang a song in *vers mesurés* accompanied by *musique mesurée* by Le Jeune, which borders on the incantatory. It celebrated the peace, happiness and prosperity of France, each verse ending with the same solemn refrain: 'ASTRES HEUREUS TOURNEZ, TOURNEZ CIEUS, TOURNE LE DESTIN'.† Never before so forcefully as in this final set of 'magnificences' was the power of art called upon to exercise its influence in averting the disasters surrounding the monarchy.

The Cardinal of Bourbon's river fête recalled that of Bayonne. A vast triumphal chariot had been prepared to bear the court to his residence at the Abbey of Saint-Germain-des-Prés. It was drawn by twenty-four little ships disguised as sea-horses, tritons, whales, sirens, tortoises, dolphins and other marine monsters, in which were concealed musicians and singers. Unfortunately the great ship refused to move and so the court was forced to go by coach to the cardinal's house, where he presented *'le plus pompeux et plus magnifique de tous'*,‡ for he had created an artificial garden with flowers and fruits in it as though it were in July or August.

In the midst of all this prodigal expenditure there is mention of the Queen Mother's fête, of workmen busy preparing a temporary room for its performance. The delays were such that it was never apparently performed, being finally postponed until some subsequent date. Ironically Catherine's life-work in festival was to find expression in the entertainment presented by her daughter-in-law, Louise of Lorraine. The *Balet Comique de la Reyne* was the only one of the Joyeuse 'magnificences' to find itself in print in full with illustrations and music. The text was by La Chesnaye, the music by the Sieur de Beaulieu, the scenery by a certain Jacques Patin, while the whole was planned and directed by Baltasar de Beaujoyeulx, who had been responsible for the *Ballet of the Provinces of France* in 1573.

14   The illustrations accurately evoke the occasion. At one end of the crowded hall sat the royal family, centring on the King with the Queen Mother, clearly visible from the rear with her diaphanous mourning veils, to his right. Opposite them, at the far end of the room, was an artificial

★'... like a large summer sun.'
†'TURN, OH HAPPY STARS, TURN, OH HEAVENS, TURN FATE.'
‡'... the most stately and most magnificent of all.'

115 *Entry of the Tritons*

garden framed by a triple arch of trellis. From the flanking arches issued the chariots and allegorical personages who were to make up the action of the ballet, while in the centre Circe, the wicked enchantress, sat enthroned. To the left of the hall was the *voûte dorée*, a star-bespangled cloud at ground level containing groups of musicians and singers. Opposite, to the right, there was a boscage in which sat Pan and behind which was a grotto full of more musicians. Above, but not indicated in the engraving of the scene, there was a cloud suspended from the ceiling.

The moral meaning of the entertainment about to be enacted was the familiar allegorical exposition of the Circe fable as found in one of the standard Renaissance mythological manuals, Natale Conti's *Mythologiae*. Circe, the daughter of Perseus and the Sun, lured men to vice, to a life of the passions that transformed them into beasts. This enchantress thus represented the passions: lasciviousness, drunkenness, cruelty, avarice, ambition, all the vices to which men, devoid of the guidance of reason, are drawn. The action was to be a moral struggle of Virtue versus Vice, of the vanquishing of Vice by the triumph of Reason and the Rational Soul. In short, the ballet was a moral debate on the lines of many we know to have taken place in the Palace Academy during the reign of Henry III.

The performance opened with a gentleman escaping from the bondage of Circe and appealing to the King to deliver him. At this point Circe bestirred herself from her garden and issued forth to harangue the royal family in fury and return once more to the far end of the room. The plot of Man struggling to free himself from the power of the passions was thus

Le Balet Comique de la Reyne, 1581 (114–21):
LEFT 114 *The Salle de Bourbon*

116 *Entry of the Sirens*

stated in this initial encounter. This was to be acted out in a series of
entrées by various mythological creatures embodying abstract forces that
successively try to vanquish the power of Circe. The first was of water
deities. Six tritons and three sirens escorted into the hall a pageant car like
a fountain drawn by sea-horses upon which sat Queen Louise and her
ladies, elaborately bejewelled, as naiads, accompanied by Glaucus and
Tethys. The sirens sang a song in *musique mesurée* praising the King and
toured the hall. They then escorted the fountain chariot up to the King and
a song followed in praise of Queen Louise, succeeded by a second by
Glaucus and Tethys complaining of the evils of Circe. Then ten violinists
entered the room, the ladies descended from their chariot and danced a
ballet of thirteen geometric figures, expressing, we are told, the mysteries
of number. These revels were at length rudely interrupted by Circe, who
rushed out from her garden and turned the dancers and musicians to stone.
Suddenly a clap of thunder was heard and from the cloud above the hall
Mercury descended, singing of his role as the messenger of the gods and
the teacher to men of science and the arts. The moment recalled that of his
arrival a decade before in the ill-starred *Paradis d'Amour*. Mercury carried
the juice of the moly herb, which had the power to cure minds that have
abandoned virtue. Having been sprinkled with the herb the performers
resumed their ballet, only to be turned to stone once again by Circe, who
issued from her garden. She mocked the naiads who cherished the ancient
Golden Age virtues and she led them off, together with Mercury, to be her
slaves. The first sequence of the *Balet* ended with the vices triumphant, for
man's intelligence manifested in the arts and sciences must be guided by
Reason and not by Passion.

115
116
117

In the second part the forces of nature challenged the power of Circe. As before the sequence opened with deities entering, this time eight satyrs who toured the hall singing a song in praise of Henry III. These were followed by a pageant car like an oak wood in which sat four dryads, who recounted the evils of Circe and called on Pan in his grotto to rescue her slaves. Both dryads and satyrs grouped themselves round his grotto but to no avail, for Pan, the universal world of nature, could not resist the powers of Circe.

118 *Entry of the Satyrs*

119 *Entry of the Dryads*

The scene was now set for the final battle. As in the case of the previous *entrées* it opened with a new group of characters touring the hall singing in praise of the King. This time it was the four Cardinal Virtues, Prudence, Fortitude, Justice and Temperance, who said that as the King was the embodiment of themselves it was he who would defeat Circe. The Virtues invoked Minerva, Goddess of Reason and Wisdom, who entered in a chariot drawn by dragons and made her progress down the length of the hall towards the King escorted by the Virtues. As she entered the music from the starry vault to the left was of an amazing beauty. Minerva announced that she would vanquish Circe on the King's behalf and invoked her father Jupiter to aid her. Once again there was a tremendous thunderclap and this time the whole cloud slowly descended from the ceiling bearing Jupiter. At this moment the *Balet* reached its musical apogee, for no less than forty musicians and singers in the *voûte dorée* sang forth:

> O bien heureux le ciel qui de ses feux nouveaux
> Ialoux effacera tous les astres flambeaux
> O bien heureux encor sous ces princes la terre
> O bien heureux aussy la nauire Francoys
> Esclairé de ses feux, bien heureux leurs loix
> Qui banniront d'icy les vices et la guerre.★

The song is of the wisdom and virtue of the kings of France in banishing war and advancing virtue. With the arrival of Jupiter the final assault on Circe began. Pan and the satyrs, the natural powers, under the direction of Minerva and the Virtues, embodying Reason and Wisdom, and aided by Jupiter, the father of the gods, advanced on the garden of the enchantress and broke her power, presenting her magic wand to the onlooking Henry III.

This triumph was celebrated in a ballet of forty geometric figures by the newly released naiads. The breaking and re-forming of the figures expressed the mutation of the elements and seasons, each single figure stating an eternal truth in geometric form. Finally the ladies presented devices to certain of the spectators. Queen Louise gave the King one depicting a dolphin, an allusion to the hoped-for birth of a Dauphin.

In this entertainment the *ballet de cour* is fully realized. We can trace in the entertainment imagery and forms from previous sets of 'magnifi-

★ Oh happy the heaven that with its new fires/will jealously outshine all the flaming stars/Oh happy yet the earth ruled over by these princes/Oh happy too the good ship France/Illuminated by its fires, happy their laws/That will banish vices and wars.

cences' all the way back to Chenonceaux and beyond to late medieval forms of masquerading and mumming. Scattered scenery is of the sort used for indoor combats such as in *Le Paradis d'Amour*; the element of combat, typified in the fight of Virtues and Vices, recalls the tradition of jousts; the marine mythology of tritons, sirens and naiads was a familiar ingredient of Valois festivals; pageant cars depicting rocks, trees and fountains were features of late medieval entertainments; choreographed dances had been first imported from Italy. All these elements are welded together into a coherent harmony of plot and dramatic denouement in the *Balet Comique*. The entertainment as a whole also reflects the aims of the academies in reviving both ancient music and dancing. And, as in the case of all previous French court spectacle, the real meaning of the ballet was political. It enacts the dramas and dilemma of the French Crown. Circe not only represents the passions, she is the evil of civil war that has wrecked the peace of the realm. Through his practice of virtue and under the guidance of reason it is predicted that Henry III will vanquish this phantom of war.

Nothing could have been more optimistic and further from political realities than the Joyeuse 'magnificences' that were the final glorious swan song of Valois court festival art. After them the rule of Henry III descends into endless eccentricities and excesses. He was surrounded by favourites, indifferent to financial ruin, and obsessed by extremes of Counter-Reformation piety. The image of the court in his last years was to be one of riotous extravagance alternating with wild penitence. The streets were now filled with processions of the King and Queen in penitential guise attended by figures of the Virtues imploring heaven that an heir be born. All was to no avail. In June 1584 Alençon, Henry's brother and the heir apparent, died, and his decease forced the ultimate issue of the succession. The Crown was isolated as never before, with a Protestant, Henry of Navarre, as heir. In September the Guise, who had been drawn momentarily back into the royal circle by the Joyeuse marriage, met at Nancy and formed a league. The next year the Holy League became an established fact. Ultra-Catholic and with direct support from Spain, it held that the Crown could not be inherited by a heretic and that the true heir was the old Cardinal of Bourbon. With this darkness begins to enfold the last years of the Valois dynasty. The united family was no more. Marguerite deserted Navarre and joined the League, much to the horror of her

120 *Entry of the four Cardinal Virtues*

mother. In July 1585 Catherine came to terms with the Leaguers in the Treaty of Nemours and, for the first time, the Crown rescinded the edict that had always guaranteed the Huguenots a degree of protection and tolerance for the practice of their faith. Once more there was war. In 1588 the League drove the King from Paris and forced him to summon a meeting of the Estates General at Blois. In December 1588 Henry III made a last desperate attempt to throw off the Guise and had both the Cardinal and his brother the Duke murdered, an action that canonized them in the eyes of the Catholic Leaguers. Poor Catherine died on 5 January 1589 and her son was assassinated by a Leaguer seven months later. With this darkness falls on what had been the most brilliant and cultivated court in Europe. For several years there was to be no king of France and the kingdom was rent by the worst and most savage of all the wars, that between the heir Henry of Navarre and the Catholic League.

In the troubled and terrible years that followed the assassination the art of festival almost died. For the transmission of the new art of *ballet de cour* into the next century one must study the simple ballets presented by Henry IV's sister, Catherine, at the little court she held at Béarn. There, in the midst of a war in which it seemed that the French monarchy was about to disappear for ever, ballets were danced before her expressing in simpler terms the same hopes and fears that her namesake in happier days had embodied in her 'magnificences'. On 23 August 1592 a ballet was danced at Pau. Four knights, two Béarnais and two French, fought for and in defence of marriage before Madame, a debate stopped by the descent of Mercury, who expressed Jupiter's rage at this combat. The plot of the ballet was simple in its evolution, with a dance of four nymphs and a triumph of Cupid, Love reconciling the knights, and it closed with predictions of Madame's own marriage, allied to hopes of peace for France and the birth of an heir. As of old the Béarnais and French knights are Protestants and Catholics, and the ballet's theme is reconciliation through love, which will bring longed-for peace once more. It recalls all that Catherine de'Medici's life work in festivals had stood for.

In the *Ballet of Medea*, the year after, a nymph appears before Catherine and her brother, the King, and begs her come to the aid of France who is cruelly ravaged by a goddess, the enchantress Medea, who reveals herself attended by two Spanish knights, the arms of Spain above her and those of France and Navarre cast at her feet. Two nymphs enter and dance a ballet until they stop before Medea and make a speech bemoaning the Spanish triumph over the *fleur de lys*. Next two French knights appear and eventually consult a sybil, who prophesies a saviour in the figure of Henry IV. A combat follows in which the French knights defeat the Spaniards and lead them prisoner before Henry IV, while Medea reluctantly does obeisance to his sister, Catherine. The victory is expressed in a final ballet by the knights and nymphs. In these poverty-stricken provincial productions with the minimum of scenery, with the fewest possible performers and devoid of the splendour of old, the art of *ballet de cour* created under the auspices of that genius of the Renaissance court fête, Catherine de'Medici, trickled its lonely course into the next century, eventually to reveal itself in a new glory in the court spectacles of *le Roi Soleil*.

121 *The Chariot of Minerva*

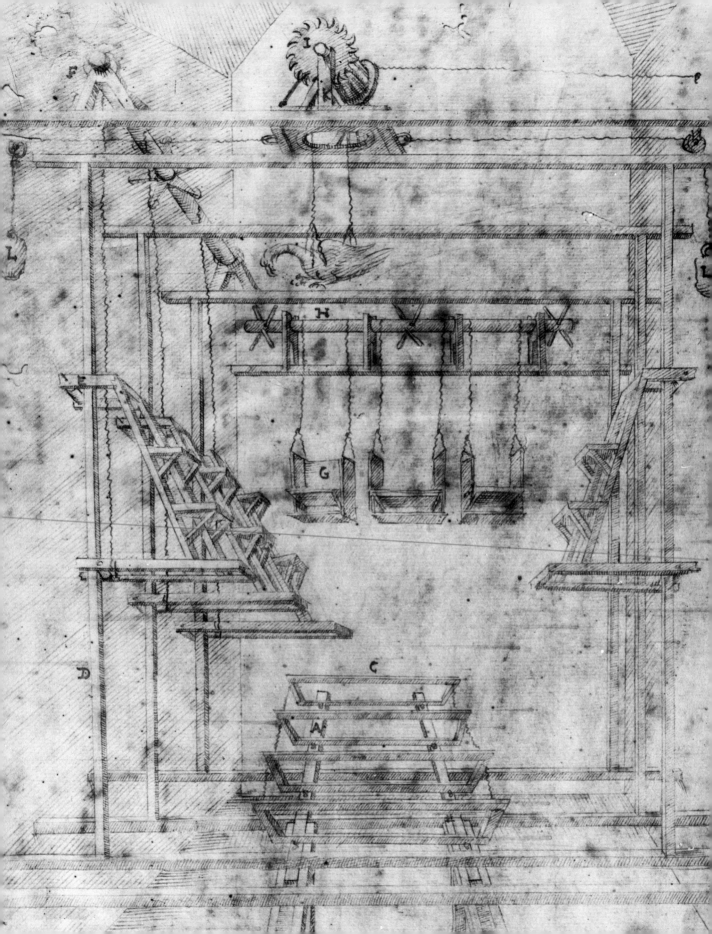

5 *A Medici Maecenas*

THE GRAND DUKE FERDINAND

Bastiano de'Rossi in his account of the most celebrated spectacle of the reign of the Grand Duke Ferdinand of Tuscany, the intermezzi of 1589, opens by praising Medicean magnificence. He begins by citing Cosimo Vecchio as an *exemplum* of this virtue, manifested in his numerous public buildings. He then goes on to recall Medici fêtes: the famous *giostra* of Lorenzo the Magnificent, the festivals of Pope Leo X and the marriage festivities of Lorenzo de'Medici to Maddelena of France. When he comes to the Grand Dukes he sees them too as exponents of this virtue in their spectacles and building projects. Cosimo I had created Cosmopolis on the island of Elba, the Fortezza di San Martino in Mugello and the Città del Sole in the Romagna, besides presiding over the splendours of both his son's and his own nuptials. Francesco, his eldest son, followed the tradition laid down by his father. His liberality was manifested in princely villas and in the development of the port of Livorno. His court fêtes were brilliant also, Bastiano relates, but none is mentioned, for the most famous was the *Sbarra* of 1579 to celebrate his notorious marriage to his mistress, Bianca Capello, a lady loathed by his successor, his brother, the Grand Duke Ferdinand. To de'Rossi, however, Ferdinand de'Medici's festivals already seemed, two years after his accession, to eclipse all that had gone before, being of an 'unheard-of marvel and wonder'. A funeral oration even more vividly casts this Grand Duke as the presiding genius over memorable fêtes. Hymning the splendour of his court it proceeds to laud that of

123 Artist unknown, *The Grand Duke Ferdinand of Tuscany*

> ... the entertainments, the spectacles, which ... were always grand, always pompous, always marvellous, always regal. ... The superb *apparati*, the stately shows, the artful devices of inestimable cost, the marvellous spectacles, which not only surpassed the universal expectation of everyone, but the imagination of the most expert, and the most wise, not only could they not conceive such things in their minds before their execution, but having seen them and seen them again, were still unable to. The expense was incredible, the artifice unimaginable, the invention of the noblest. ...

As in the case of Catherine de'Medici, court spectacle was a deliberate part of the policy of the Grand Dukes of Tuscany.

Medici festivals in the grand-ducal period were motivated by different problems from those confronting the Habsburg and Valois dynasties. The Medici were *nouveaux*, and each series of fêtes was designed to enhance the grandeur of this infant dynasty, which due to its role as bankers was able

OPPOSITE 122 *Back stage at the Teatro Farnese. View of the stage machinery located in the gridiron, with suspended seats and flanking platforms that could be raised or lowered by means of a windlass*

169

to buy its way into alliances with the ruling houses of Europe. Charles V had restored the Medici to power in Florence in 1529 and subsequently created Alessandro de'Medici Duke in 1531. Cosimo, his successor, remained true to the imperial alliance and for this he was richly rewarded. He was given a Spanish bride, Eleanor of Toledo, daughter of the Viceroy of Naples, in 1539; was handed Siena in 1557; and, as a wife for his eldest son, Francesco, received an Austrian Archduchess, Joanna, sister to the Emperor Maximilian II, in 1565. This match represented a diplomatic triumph for the Medici family and further consolidated their position as one of the ruling houses of Europe. At the right moment the skilful Cosimo had turned pro-papal and, in return, had had the title of Grand Duke bestowed on him by Pius V. Medici rule in the late sixteenth century was therefore directed towards the deliberate suppression of any lingering republican traditions within Florence and the promotion of autocratic principles. Under the influence of Eleanor of Toledo Spanish court etiquette was introduced and society became gradually more feudalized. The new aristocracy, owing their status to the Medici, overshadowed the senators, with a consequent division between those who sought civic as against court honours. The gradual emergence of the Medici as a ruling dynasty owed much to a deliberate artistic policy that was expressed in vast cycles of frescoes within their palaces and villas glorifying events in the family's history, in erecting public monuments and statues in their own honour, and in the periodic staging of stupendous fêtes in which every event in the life of the Medici family was presented as being of universal import.

123   The Grand Duke Ferdinand was Cosimo's second son. At the age of fourteen he had been made a cardinal and he held court in Rome until he succeeded his brother in October 1587. While in Rome he had founded the great missionary establishment, the Propaganda, and also accumulated a vast collection of classical antiquities, acquired through the dissolution of the papal collections by Counter-Reformation popes. The collection included the celebrated Venus de'Medici, the Wrestlers, the Dancing Faun and the group of Niobe and her children, all of which Ferdinand housed in the Medici villa in Rome, but later, after his accession, transferred to the Uffizi. Ferdinand had hated his brother and bitterly opposed his pro-Spanish policies, so that his accession meant a total volte-face in the political attitudes of the state of Tuscany. As cardinal he had always maintained

170

a secret correspondence with Catherine de'Medici, and when he became Grand Duke in 1587 it meant a dramatic reversal of policies from pro-Habsburg to pro-Valois. This ironically occurred at a moment when the fortunes of the French royal house were at their lowest ebb.

Ferdinand announced the nature of his rule by his *impresa*, a swarm of bees encompassing their queen and the motto *Majestate Tantum*, signifying that his government should be just and temperate and one that would enable his people to lay up wealth as bees stored honey. He opened his reign by burying his brother with great splendour, pardoning his ministers, keeping some and recalling a number of his father's. In a Europe rent by religious war and economic disorder the state of Tuscany under the liberal rule of Ferdinand assumed an important place in European politics in the last two decades of the sixteenth century. The Grand Dukes remained bankers and although Florentine banking had suffered a severe setback when Spain had declared its bankruptcy in 1580, this had not upset the Medici bank. Central to grand-ducal policy was the creation and enlargement of the port of Livorno, where the Grand Dukes proclaimed complete religious toleration. To it flocked both Protestant and Catholic English, Huguenots from Marseilles, Portuguese Jews, Flemings, merchants and traders of every nation seeking shelter from the political and religious disorder of their own countries. Together with Genoa, Livorno became the leading port in the Mediterranean at the close of the sixteenth century. Similarly there was an encouragement of agriculture manifested in the draining of the Valdichiana, and there was a militant naval policy both in the activities of the grand-ducal order, the Knights of St Stephen, in sweeping the seas of the Infidel, and in voyages of discovery, which Ferdinand seriously supported and encouraged. The Medici family were the foremost bankers and traders and their fabulous wealth was reflected in the sumptuous richness of their court. While commerce and agriculture flourished, art and science were promoted. The grand-ducal gardens were the most marvellous in Tuscany, Ferdinand establishing a botanical garden in 1593. The ablest physicians were attracted to teach medicine at Pisa, where Galileo was professor of mathematics from 1589 to 1592. In addition, the Medici art collections were thrown open to public view and the architect Buontalenti created the Tribunà with its ceiling of mother-of-pearl set in gilded gesso and its pavement inlaid with coloured marbles. The Grand Duke also collected the rarest manuscripts from Egypt, Persia and Ethiopia for his library and his chapel was staffed by some of the greatest singers and composers of the day. The reign of the Grand Duke Ferdinand was indeed a golden age for Tuscany.

Even by the close of 1587 Ferdinand had arranged that he should marry Christina, Catherine de' Medici's grand-daughter, then aged twenty-two. Catherine de' Medici and Henry III sent Monsieur Albin to Florence and maintained the negotiations via Orazio Rucellai. When news reached Madrid of the impending alliance Philip II was furious and countered with alternative offers of an Austrian archduchess or a princess of Braganza, both of which were promptly rejected by Ferdinand. The King of Spain's annoyance was increased by the Duke's demand that Spanish military governors should be relieved of their posts in Tuscany and that the vast debts owing to the Medici bank should be repaid. In October Orazio Rucellai arrived at the French court to conclude the marriage negotiations. Christina came with a dowry of 600,000 crowns, 50,000 in jewels, together with the renunciation of claims on Medicean property by Catherine and a transfer to Christina of the Queen Mother's claims to the Duchy of Urbino. On the day on which magnificent jewels arrived at the French court for the bride, the Duke of Guise was assassinated by order of the King. This, together with the death of Catherine herself on 5 January 1589, delayed the departure of the bride. 'Happy are you my niece,' said Henry III, 'for you will be in a peaceful land and not see the ruin of my poor kingdom.' On 27 February the *fiançailles* took place at Cheverny and the day after Christina left on her journey. The collapse of royal power was such that an army was needed to conduct the bride and her train in safety to Marseilles, which had declared itself a republic. On 23 April the flotilla bearing the new Grand Duchess anchored at Livorno. Travelling via Pisa to the Medici villa of Poggio a Caiano Christina met her husband for the first time and on 30 April the bride made her solemn entry into Florence.

Everything for the Medici depended on the creation of precedents. The entry of Joanna of Austria into Florence in 1565 had caused considerable work, as nothing comparable had been done since 1539 on the occasion of Eleanor of Toledo's entry. In 1565 the status of the Medici was considerably different from what it had been twenty-six years before, so Cosimo instructed Vincenzo Borghini to undertake research into the conventions of the royal entry. Borghini's elaborate report still survives. He mainly concludes that there were three types of entry: the first that of a prince into

124 Artist unknown, *Christina of Lorraine, Grand Duchess of Tuscany*

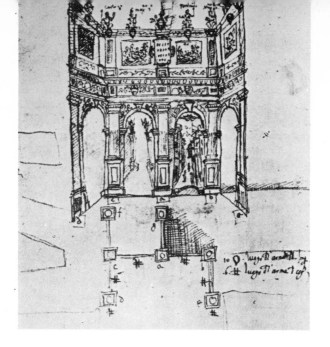

125 Vincenzo Borghini, *Sketch of an arch for Joanna of Austria's Entry into Florence, 1565*

a city of his own; the second that of a prince into a city belonging to another ruler; and the third an entry in connection with a marriage. The result was a pattern of themes for the reception of a Medici bride that was to be enacted many times in the next century. Borghini's programme began with an arch dedicated to the city of Florence, next a decoration to Hymen, god of marriage, an arch celebrating the bride's own family, an amphitheatre lauding the groom's family and, finally, three arches expressing the wisdom and magnanimity of Duke Cosimo's rule. This was embodied in an arch devoted to *Religione*, which led on to one on the subject of *Prudenza Civile* closing with *Tranquillità Pubblica* which, in tribute to the Medici, was found to reside in the Palazzo Vecchio.

Christina took the same route into Florence as the one taken by Joanna twenty-four years before. The entry this time was arranged under the direction of Niccolò Gaddi, who had total control of *le invenzioni*, which basically elaborated themes begun in the 1565 entry. Pietro Angelio da Barga wrote the inscriptions and verses and a vast team of architects, sculptors and painters laboured upon it. The underlying programme for the street decorations is revealed by Gaddi in his commentary on the last arch, when he writes that the story told was 'the foundation and the restoration of the city of Florence, and its coming to honour and greatness, through such and so many victories, and its coming to its supreme height, and to a royal state'. This entailed a deliberate presentation, or rather distortion, of Florentine history as an inevitable progression from republican rudeness to monarchical perfection, with the Medici presented as the preordained ultimate power on account of their military prowess, civic virtue, munificence and liberality.

Christina of Lorraine's Entry into Florence, 1589 (126–31):
126 *Arch of the city of Florence*

The first arch, following the pattern of Joanna's entry, was dedicated to the city of Florence and its history. Scenes included the founding of Florence by the imperial triumvirate of Augustus, Anthony and Lepidus, its second foundation by Charlemagne, the union of Florence and Fiesole leading to a climax in a canvas by Alessandro Allori depicting Florence and her dependants. The city was significantly attired 'in a regal habit, similar to that worn by the Grand Dukes' and her cloak was embroidered with the Medici arms.

The Medici theme was further developed in the second arch, which celebrated previous Medici marriages and told the story of the present one. In a Europe where it seemed that the French monarchy was at its nadir, Christina was greeted by a huge canvas in the centre of which Catherine de'Medici was seated in great splendour surrounded by famous members

175

127 *The marriage of Catherine de' Medici*

128 *Christina takes leave of her family*

of the Medici family: Popes Leo X and Clement VII, the Cardinals Ippolito and Giovanni de'Medici, the Duke Alessandro, the Grand Dukes Cosimo and Francesco, arrayed in their robes with ducal crowns, and the whole French royal family, including all to whom they were married, except Philip II of Spain, husband of Catherine's daughter Elizabeth. In this astounding tableau Ferdinand made a public statement of his policy and exalted his family as equals of the French royal house, casting Catherine in the role of a kind of grandmother of Europe. Further canvases celebrated previous French marriages, of Catherine to Henry II, and of Duke Charles of Lorraine to Claude of France, while events in this bride's life were also depicted, including her parting from her family and her embarkation from Marseilles.

The exaltation of the Medici by a careful juxtaposition with other grander figures was elaborated on the Ponte Sta Trinità, on which four statues were erected of founders of Florence along with Cosimo Vecchio and Cosimo, the first Grand Duke. Here the two Medici were presented as 'founders' within this present age. There followed the customary arch dedicated to the bride's family, this time the house of Lorraine, descendants of the crusading King of Jerusalem, Geoffrey of Boulogne, and a decoration tactfully in praise of Charles V (who had restored the Medici to power in Florence) and Philip II (who decidedly did not approve of the marriage) with large paintings of the battles of Linz and Lepanto, to both of which victories against the Turk Duke Cosimo had contributed. As the

127

128

129

176

129 *Christina embarks from Marseilles*

130 *Decoration in praise of Duke Cosimo*

bride advanced through the streets ever closer to the Palazzo Vecchio the glorification of the groom's family intensified. The virtues of a good ruler that had formed so substantial a part of the 1565 entry were abandoned in favour of outright apotheosis. In one Cosimo and Eleanor were shown as golden statues surrounded by their family. Even the unpopular Francesco was suddenly recorded as 'a true mirror of the just and temperate life'. Three scenes depicted the crucial events in Cosimo's life: Pius IV authorizing the creation of the establishment of the Order of St Stephen; Cosimo organizing the fortification of Tuscan cities; and, as a climax, his creation as Duke on 9 January 1537.

The decoration before the palace contained the real crux of the entry. One scene showed Cosimo crowned Grand Duke by Pius V, another Francesco enthroned amid his court and magistrates – a gesture towards the city – while in the centre there was perhaps the most significant statement about Medici rule in the entire entry. In the midst of a large canvas sat Tuscany, arrayed in the grand-ducal mantle, her crown being taken away from her by the pagan Etruscan King Porsenna, while Cosimo leant forward to crown her yet again. The Medici Grand Dukes are here presented as restoring Tuscany to her ancient purity of monarchical rule, made proper because the Medici are monuments to Christian piety whereas Porsenna was one to idolatry. Behind him stood an altar adorned with pagan religious vessels. This extraordinary group was completed by Siena, in a robe embroidered with Medici *palle*, and by Tuscany presenting her

177

131 *The Apotheosis of Tuscany*

sceptre to Florence in a robe 'similar to that of the Grand Dukes'. In this way, by means of allegorical tableaux and subtle juxtaposition of historical personages, the Medici family, who less than a hundred years before had been one of many rich mercantile families within Florence, was presented as the heirs of ancient kings, as the equals of the house of Valois, as the pre-ordained savours of Florence, whose republican period was now viewed as an imperfection and prelude to the perfect rule of Medici autocracy. The decorations in the streets of Florence were no doubt intended to be more meaningful to its inhabitants than to the arriving bride.

The court now embarked on a cycle of fêtes that stretched over some three weeks, the climax of which were the celebrated intermezzi of 1589, a landmark in the origins of opera and in the history of theatrical production. As in the case of the *Balet Comique de la Reyne*, the intermezzi were produced under the influence of humanist theories concerning music and spectacle and, as in the case of the *Balet Comique* also, they both ended in representing a compromise between the demands of the learned and those of a courtly audience. The music in the *Balet Comique* was strongly in the mood of *musique mesurée à l'antique* promoted by de Baïf's Academy, but it was minus regular antique metre and the dance tunes were devoid of humanist influence at all. None the less the central humanist position in which music was to be the handmaid of poetry and thus recapture ancient 'effects' was the dominant one. In the intermezzi for Christina the same problems were faced and the same solutions reached. In order to understand the intermezzi for Christina, however, we must first reconnoitre back in time to a tradition very different from that of the *ballet de cour*.

The tradition of intermezzi went back to the close of the fifteenth century, to Poliziano's *Orfeo* at Ferrara and Niccolò da Coreggio's *Cefalo*. These were mythological interludes inserted between the acts of court plays and also into other forms of fêtes staged to mark great occasions, ballets, tournaments and other chivalrous *divertissements*. At the Medici court these were developed into a major artistic phenomenon with elaborate visual spectacle allied to grandiose vocal and instrumental music. There was a series of seven intermezzi on the occasion of Cosimo's marriage to Eleanor of Toledo in 1539. These were inserted into Antonio Landi's play *Il Commodo* and were written by Giovanbattista Strozzi with music by Corteccia and produced under the direction of Pier Francesco Giamballari. The themes were related to the play but each remained a separate piece unconnected with those before or after it. As the century progressed, and under the impact of late Renaissance humanism, intermezzi were to gain thematic unity. Those of 1539 took place within the confines of an elaborate perspective stage setting for the comedy. There were classical rustic entrées of shepherds, of sirens, of Silenus and of nymphs who sang songs. Twenty-six years later the intermezzi for *La Cofanaria* with scenery by Vasari and Timante did not substantially develop this format. Again there was a *prospettiva* for the *commedia*, this time of Florence, and again the intermezzi took place within it, the only new effects being the introduction of cloud visions and an extensive use of trap-

132 Bernardo Buontalenti, *Design for the Doric Harmony in the Prologue to the intermezzi, 1589*

133 *The setting for the play 'La Pellegrina', 1589 (?)*

doors for the entry of demons and for the raising and lowering of props such as mountains. There was an advance in the introduction of a unity of theme, all being concerned with episodes from the life of Cupid and Psyche, whose union at the close was metamorphosed into that of the onlooking bride and groom, Joanna of Austria and Francesco de' Medici.

Twenty-four years divide this from Girolamo Bargagli's play *La Pellegrina*, which was performed on 2 May 1589 in the Uffizi theatre and began with a prologue to the first of the celebrated intermezzi. The front curtain parted to reveal a Doric temple and above it a cloud, surrounded by rays of light, which slowly descended to the ground. On this rode the Doric Harmony, singing of her descent to mortals and especially to the bridal couple, this *'nuova Minerva'* and her *'forte Alcide'*. At the close of the first act, which was set in the usual perspective stage setting of a town, this time Pisa, the prologue was carried to fruition in a representation of the Harmony of the Spheres according to Platonic cosmology, and in particular as described in the tenth book of the *Republic*. The *prospettiva* of Pisa, the setting for the first act of the play, was suddenly covered with star-spangled clouds. Eight Platonic sirens plus two more of the ninth and tenth sphere sat on clouds telling how they had forsaken the heavens to sing the praises of the bride. On a central cloud sat Necessity on a throne with a diamond spindle of the cosmos between her knees. She was at-

132

133

135

Plate XI

RIGHT XI Bernardo Buontalenti, *Design for Necessity and the Fates for the first intermezzo, 1589*

OVERLEAF
134 Bernardo Buontalenti, *Design for the sixth intermezzo, 1589. The Assembly of the Gods*

180

135 *The first intermezzo, 1589. The Harmony of the Spheres*

late XIIa

tended by the three Parcae or Fates and they in turn were flanked by clouds bearing the seven planets and Astraea, whose advent on earth signalled the return of the Golden Age. Above were twelve heroes and heroines, each pair embodying virtues attributed to the onlooking couple. Both sirens and the planets joined in a dialogue describing the joy of the cosmos at so auspicious an alliance and as the clouds arose from the lower part of the stage sunlight streamed in, while above night approached. A concluding madrigal expressed hopes of 'glorious heroes' as a result of the match. As the cloud vision faded the stage was filled with sunlight, revealing the setting for Act Two of *La Pellegrina*, the *prospettiva* of the city of Pisa.

This extraordinary scene combined a learned public exposition of a programme for musical reform with compliments to the bride and groom. The musical ideas stem from the *Camerata Fiorentina dei Bardi*, which was presided over by Giovanni de'Bardi, Conte di Vernio, humanist and Maecenas, and which, between the years 1576 and 1582, presented a pro-

OPPOSITE ABOVE
XII Bernardo Buontalenti, *Design for Apollo slaying the Python for the third of the intermezzi, 1589*
BELOW Bernardo Buontalenti, *Design for Mercury, Apollo, Jupiter and Astraea in the first of the intermezzi, 1589*

185

gramme for the revival of Greek tragedy together with the use of music.
Within this circle of reformers moved Piero Strozzi who, together with
Giovanni de'Bardi, was one of the closest of Galileo's collaborators in the
search 'towards the imitation by song of that which is spoken', a quest that
led to the earliest operas. Already in the *Sbarra* of 1579 to celebrate the
wedding of Bianca Capello to Francesco de'Medici this had been introduced into court spectacle. One of the surviving madrigals is one in which
a soprano sang a poetic text, following its inflexions to a bass accompani-
ment.

The principles of the *Camerata Fiorentina* probably made themselves even
more strongly felt on the occasion of the intermezzi of 1586 on the marriage of Virginia de'Medici to Cesare d'Este. Little is known about the
visual appearance or the musical content of this spectacle, but the team was
largely that of 1589. Count Bardi wrote the comedy, *L'Amico Fido*,
furnished the themes for the six intermezzi and composed the music for
the last of them. Bernardo Buontalenti, the great architect and engineer,
not only constructed a permanent *salle des fêtes*, a *teatro* that can be seen in
Callot's engraving of *La Liberazione di Terreno* some thirty years later, but
designed the sets and costumes. The cost was stupendous, some 25,000
scudi, and more than four hundred workmen are said to have been involved in the actual production. Each interlude was related in theme to the
marriage and its repertory of themes and décor was in many ways a dress-
rehearsal for 1589. Vast advances in theatrical engineering had been
achieved. Instead of a cloud being lowered and then pulled up again, it was
now possible to blow it from the stage at ground level. In the first intermezzo Jupiter and the gods celebrated the return of the Golden Age
through the marriage, and Jove sent his blessings to earth to inaugurate the
new era. In the second the audience was led to the realms of classical hell,
where the evils lamented their defeat, and the story was continued in the
third, where Spring arrived – in the Golden Age Spring is perpetual – and
in the fourth, where the rejoicings of earth were extended to the sea, with
Neptune calming the waves and sea-deities singing in praise of the
nuptials. Juno, goddess of marriage, showered her blessings in the fifth and
the happiness of earth and heaven were localized in the final intermezzo, in
which shepherds and shepherdesses in Tuscan costume danced in triumph.

The intermezzi of 1589 were a result of a collaboration between
Giovanni de'Bardi, Ottavio Rinuccini, Giovanbattista Strozzi and Laura
Guidiccioni. Music was by musicians of the grand-ducal chapel, Cristo-

7

136 *The second intermezzo, 1589. The Contest of the Pierides and Muses*

fano Malvezzi and Luca Marenzio, and three young, advanced composers, Emilio de'Cavalieri, Giulio Caccini and Jacopo Peri. Cavalieri occupied a special position because Ferdinand had appointed him superintendent of his court fêtes, and although de'Bardi was the most heavily involved he was rather a relic from the reign of the Duke's brother, Francesco, and as such less acceptable. The production was magnificent and cost 30,255 *fiorini*, 4 *lire* and 25 *soldi*. Its technical side was under the direction of Ser Jacopo de'Corsi, who instructed the detachments of men who were stationed at all points backstage: some to trim wicks and refill lamps, others to man the windlasses controlling clouds or to push back and forth shutters within their grooves for scene changes. Two hundred and eighty-six costumes were made, on which work began in October 1588. Two tailors with fifty assistants constructed them, virtually every detail having been specified by Count Bardi, and amplified by the designer

Nove Mascera: dippesta sorte:

137 Bernardo Buontalenti, *Costume design for the magpies in the second intermezzo, 1589*

Buontalenti. Every dress was an archaeological triumph, each attribute being based on a classical source.

The first intermezzo on the Doric mode was also an antiquarian triumph. Following Plato and Aristotle Bardi proclaimed the Doric mode to be the most excellent. The theme of the intermezzi of 1589 was therefore the re-creation of ancient music, of both *musica mundana* and *musica humana*. The opening intermezzo was an expression of *musica mundana* and the six intermezzi as a series elaborate the powers of music with heroic examples from Greek mythology, ending in the sixth with a representation of its gift to mankind. In the second there was enacted the contest between the Muses and Pierides set in a garden with orange and lemon trees. After the contest the prize was awarded to the Muses, following which the Pierides turned into magpies to run croaking and chattering

136

137

138 *The third intermezzo, 1589. Apollo's slaying of the Python*

138

ate XIIb

139

140

from the stage. The main scenic feat of this intermezzo was the huge mountain pulled up from below stage. In the following one Bardi re-created an ancient Greek musical festival based on a passage in Lucian's *De Saltatione* in which the people of Delphi sing Pythian songs in honour of Apollo, slayer of the dragon, the mighty battle of which actually took place before the eyes of the spectators. This was performed to music in ancient metric modes and was choreographed in five parts. In the fourth intermezzo there was a return to Platonic cosmology and an enchantress summoned up a vision opposite to the first, that is, one of disharmony, a demonic hell scene following the pattern of the previous one in 1586. In the fifth Bardi took another example of the power of ancient music, the story of Arion being rescued by a music-loving dolphin who had heard his playing before he was thrown overboard from a ship. This time

189

139 *The fourth intermezzo, 1589. The Inferno*

140 *The fifth intermezzo, 1589. The Rescue of Arion*

Buontalenti conjured up a sea-scene onto which rode Vittoria Archilei, the great soprano of the day, as Amphitrite on a shell of mother-of-pearl drawn by two dolphins and attended by tritons and naiads who sang a song in praise of the marriage. A galley with a crew of forty entered and after performing amazing feats, including striking sail in honour of the Grand Duke, the crew attacked the singing Arion, who jumped over-board. Arion next appeared playing his instrument, singing and floating through the waves on the back of a dolphin. Finally in the sixth inter-mezzo the themes of the spectacle came to a conclusion. As in the first scene the whole stage was a cloud vision, which parted to reveal an

134 Olympus of some twenty gods and Virtues. The myth to be enacted this time was derived from Plato's *Laws*. Jupiter, taking pity on humans, dispatched Harmony and Rhythm to earth so that man might obtain relief from his burdens through singing and dancing. As they descended twenty couples in pastoral dress entered, lured by the celestial music, and danced a ballet while singing a song in honour of the bridal couple.

The intermezzi, with their accent on spectacular scenic devices which left the audience '*stupiti*', were also expressions of the Renaissance exaltation of 'wonder' as an experience. Renaissance theorists based their development of spectacle on a passage in Aristotle's *Poetics*, where they read that 'the fearsome and the piteous may arise from spectacle'. For Aristotle

141 *Rigging at the Teatro Farnese with folding platforms and staircases. At the right the frame for a cloud machine suspended on ropes from pulleys attached to cross beams*

wonder is the end of poetry and as drama is a form of poetry its end too is to evoke wonder in the minds of the onlookers. So in the hands of Renaissance dramatic theorists wonder expressed in terms of sheer visual spectacle gradually assumes an important place in drama, something aided by the knowledge, through Vitruvius, that stage scenery had been used in the theatres of classical antiquity. Vitruvius describes the use of *periaktoi*, revolving triangular frames to change scene, but later, in a chapter on machines and engines, hints that elaborate machinery may have been a feature of the antique drama. Such things, he wrote, 'please the eye of people'.

This concern with stage machinery and engines was taken a step further by Sebastiano Serlio in his *Architettura*, published in 1545, which includes the celebrated wood engravings of three types of play setting, the tragic, comic and satyric, but also contains important passages on the theory of spectacle:

Among all the things that may bee made by mens hands, thereby to yeeld admiration, pleasure to sight, and to content the fantasies of men; I think it is placing of a Scene, as it is shewed to your sight, where a man in a small place may see built by Carpenters or Masons, skilfull in Perspective work, great Palaces, large Temples, and divers Houses, both neere and farre off; broad places filled with Houses, long streets crost with other ways: tryumphant Arches, high Pillars or Columnes, Piramides, Obeliscens, and a thousand fayre things and buildings, adorned with innumerable lights. ... There you may see the bright shining Moone ascending only with her hornes, and already risen up, before the spectators are ware of, or once saw it ascend. In some other Scenes you may see the rising of the Sunne with his course about the world: and at the ending of the Comedie, you may see it goe downe most artifically, where at many beholders have been abasht. And when occasion serveth, you shall by Arte see a God descending downe from Heaven: you also see some Comets and Stars shoot in the skyes ... which things, as occasion serveth, are so pleasant to mens eyes, that a man could not see fairer with mens hands.

The effects demanded for Renaissance court spectacle were obtainable only because of staggering developments within the field of mechanics during the sixteenth century. We have to go a little forward in time to find drawings that give us any idea of the astounding engineering backstage that produced these seemingly miraculous visual effects. Federigo Zuccaro, the Roman Mannerist painter and a textbook Neo-Platonist, waxes lyrical at the sight of the machines backstage at Mantua in 1608 which

122
141

enabled man to re-create in facsimile these visions of the celestial and sublunar worlds:

It was delightful to see the windlasses mounted over the machines, the cables of optimum strength, the ropes and lines by which the machines were moved and guided, and the many stagehands who were needed to keep the apparatus in operation. Every man was at his station, and at a signal the machinery could be raised, lowered, moved, or held in a particular position. More than three hundred workers were engaged and had to be directed, which required no less experience and skill than it did foresight and reason; it must be realized that in such a situation anything might go awry and unforeseen incidents must be prevented, since one fiery spark could put an end to everything.

One senses the triumph of the apparent total control of the physical world. Some of the earliest discoveries in the field of applied science were first used in the development of the illusionistic theatre of the Platonic Idea.

Serlio also casts stupendous scenic spectacle with a powerful political and social role, for these things are manifestations of the virtue of magnificence:

This have I seene in some Scenes made by Ieronimo Genga, for the pleasure and delight of his lord and patron Francesco Maria, Duke of Urbin: wherein I saw so greate liberalitie used by the Prince, and so good a conceit in the workeman, and so good Art and proportion in things therein represented, as ever I saw in all my life before. Oh good Lord, what magnificence was there to be seene. ...

When they were based on such an ideology it is hardly surprising that the engineers and designers of these calculated visions came to occupy so important a place in late sixteenth- and early seventeenth-century courts. For the intermezzi of 1589 the Grand Duke had in his service a truly Vitruvian architect, Bernardo Buontalenti.

Such a theory of wonder based on the idea of spectacle as essential to drama, aligned to a celebration of magnificence and liberality as regal virtues, required persons able to realize these princely toys. The Renaissance architect trained in the science of the Vitruvian disciplines was a mathematician and a geometrician able to express in his work the harmonies of the universe as found in man the microcosm. His activity was a perpetual realization of such images of harmony. Bernardo Buontalenti was one in a succession of artists in the service of the Medici court whose task was to give expression to ducal magnificence. His predecessor had been Vasari, his successor was to be Giulio Parigi. Born in 1531, he had been trained at the grand-ducal court and was early associated with the

Grand Duke Francesco and shared with him a passion for things mechanical and scientific. One of the earliest anecdotes concerning Buontalenti recalls a childhood toy he made, a peep-show with a representation of the heavens together with floating angels. The history of court spectacle is closely aligned to developments in mechanics; indeed one of the earliest applications of the new discoveries in the way of machines was to theatrical peep-shows in which a court audience was filled with wonder by being presented with facsimiles of the world around them.

Buontalenti belongs to this ethos of Mannerist marvels, designing strange grottoes and automata for Francesco's villa at Pratolino. His temporary *mise en scène* for Medici baptisms, obsequies and marriages elevated the family, by means of visual reference, on to a heroic level. The designs for the 1589 intermezzi are crucial, for they are the earliest illustrations of what became a norm throughout Europe for theatrical visual experience for the next three hundred years, the proscenium arch behind which receded ranks of side wings, the vista closed by a back-shutter. Such a solution was probably reached in 1586 in the earlier series of intermezzi for which we have no certain designs but for which the Uffizi theatre was built, the architecture of which assumes such a peep-show arrangement. It is significant that this highly artificial means of visual experience and control of audience image receptivity was evolved at a court presided over by a new dynasty ever-anxious to promote itself to new levels of grandeur to conceal its bourgeois origins. Enclosed within the *teatro* of the Uffizi Palace an audience of some three thousand was to be subject time and again to some amazing visual experience glorifying the Medici in whose eyes all lines of vision met.

Musically and visually the intermezzi of 1589 take their place as one of the great landmarks of artistic creation in late sixteenth-century Europe. The threads of archaeological antiquarianism and musical reform mingle with mechanical marvels and courtly magnificence. Over the intermezzi as a series every form of musical effect was used, both traditional and revolutionary: polyphony to several choirs alternate with madrigals, the *balletto* with the *canzonetta*. But for the development of opera there were monodic songs accompanied by several instrumental groups, nascent orchestral arrangements, and the use of choirs of several parts, a device justified by the aesthetic principles of Greek tragedy. Through the engravings issued in 1592 by Epifanio d'Alfiano of the second, fourth, fifth and sixth intermezzi and those by Agostino Caracci for the first and third,

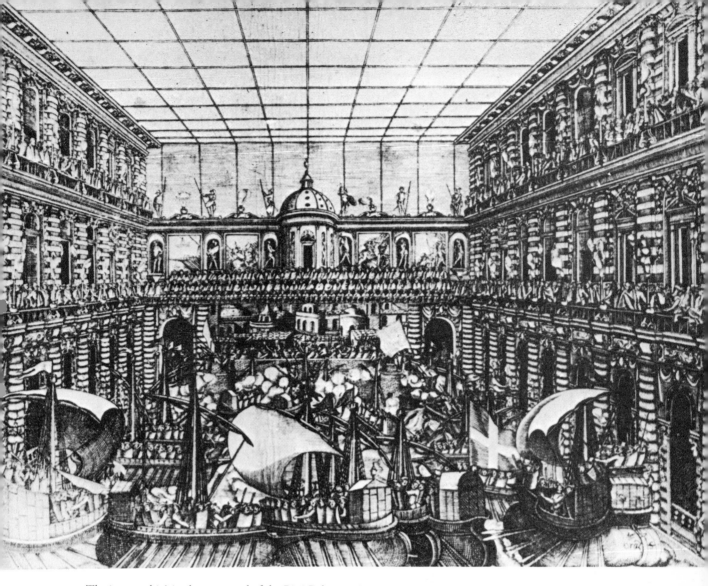

142 *The 'naumachia' in the courtyard of the Pitti Palace, 1589*

the new wonders of perspective stage spectacle, in which facsimiles of the physical world and Platonic ideas could be made apprehensible, crossed Europe. From the miraculous scenery of 1589 stemmed the Baroque theatre.

The other entertainments, save one, were minor. There was a *calcio* on 4 May in the Piazza S. Croce; the intermezzi were repeated on 6 May with a new play, *Zingara*, by the company Gelosi, animal baiting on 8 May in the Piazza S. Croce, yet a third performance of the intermezzi on 13 May with another play, *Pazzia*, a *corso al saracino* on 23 May and, finally, on the twenty-eighth a river fête. The most important of these festivals, however, took place on the eleventh, a barriers followed by a *naumachia* in the courtyard of the Pitti Palace. Little is known of the themes of this *Sbarra*, but it seems to have been basically one of Christians versus Turks, one apposite to the Tuscan court whose naval wars against the Infidel were unceasing. On the garden side a fortress had been built to be defended by Turks and there was a procession of pageant cars, or rather moveable scenery: one bearing a sorcerer, a second pulled by a dragon concealing musicians, one like Mount Etna which opened to reveal two knights. Fountains, clouds, shrubbery, animals, ships, boulders, sirens, birds and elephants paraded across the arena. Don Virginio de' Medici entered as Mars on a mountain pulled by a crocodile, but the real *coup de théâtre* was a float like a garden from which birds flew and in which the plants had been clipped into shapes like towers and pyramids or ships and horsemen. The audience, having enjoyed the marvels of the *Sbarra*, retired to feast, after which they returned to find the courtyard flooded to a depth of five feet. On this lake floated eighteen galleys, which stormed and took the Turkish fortress.

Three months after these stupendous festivals a Dominican friar assassinated Henry III and the Huguenot Henry of Navarre became in title the next King of France. True to his liberal policies the Grand Duke Ferdinand never wavered in his loyalty to the French Crown. It was indeed Medici loans that financed Henry IV's armies in the long war against the forces of the Catholic League and contributed substantially to putting him on the French throne. From the moment of his accession Ferdinand urged upon Henry IV the necessity of his conversion to Catholicism, and the Florentine court acted as mediator between the French King and Rome. Pope Clement VIII considered any proposals by Henry to change his faith merely a ruse to obtain the throne and a shallow event that would immediately after be promptly disclaimed. Henry sent the Cardinal de Gondi to Rome, but being refused admittance the Cardinal took refuge at the Florentine court. Under continued pressure from Ferdinand Henry at last agreed to change his faith in April 1593, saying that he would do so after he had defeated the Duke of Lorraine; on these grounds he was given four thousand more Swiss mercenaries and a further loan of two hundred thousand crowns by the Medici. Meanwhile Ferdinand opened negotiations with Rome on behalf of the French King by way of the Cardinal of Toledo. With the Catholic League holding a General Assembly in Paris to name a Catholic king and with the Spanish ambassador provoking them by proposing the Infanta, Henry's abjuration of Protestantism and recep-

143 Frans Pourbus, *Henry IV*

tion into the Catholic Church was accelerated, an event that finally happened on 25 July 1593. As Ferdinand had predicted, once the conversion had been achieved the collapse of the League was only a matter of time, as was also the King's recognition by the Pope.

The change in the position of the French monarchy was epitomized two years later in January 1595, when France formally declared war on Spain. Pressure from Ferdinand and from the Emperor at last forced the Pope to send Henry IV an ambassador. Shortly after that a French ambassador was allowed to proceed to Rome and the long-awaited reconciliation followed. Thenceforth the Grand Duke's efforts centred on obtaining peace, the result of which was the Treaty of Vervins in May 1598; this, like Câteau-Cambrésis in 1559, was a turning-point in the pattern of European politics. Spain and France were both bankrupt and exhausted after years of war. This meant that during the closing decade of the sixteenth century the state of Tuscany came to occupy a unique position within Europe. At peace and rich from banking, from the profits of the corn trade and from the staggering development of Livorno as an international port, the grand dukes of Tuscany enjoyed, for a brief period, a position they were never subsequently to attain.

The Treaty of Vervins laid the way open for a final coup of Medici diplomacy, another Medici bride for the French King. The divorce of Henry's wife, the brilliant Marguerite de Valois, in 1599 made possible Ferdinand's long-cherished project of marrying his niece, Marie de' Medici, then aged twenty-five, to Henry IV. This match had been mooted as long ago as 1592 by the Cardinal de Gondi, but it was not resurrected until after Henry's conversion to Catholicism. Negotiations began in 1597, by which time Henry owed Ferdinand some 1,747,147 gold crowns. The French demanded a dowry of one and a half million, but in the end accepted 600,000 crowns, 350,000 in cash and the rest deducted from the enormous royal debt. In December 1599 the marriage contract was at last signed.

The pamphlet describing the fêtes for the marriage sets the event within vistas of universal peace. Marie's marriage was made public within Florence on 30 April, the day that Christina had entered the city as a bride eleven years before. Due to various delays the marriage did not actually take place until 5 October, when the Cardinal Aldobrandini, the papal legate, married the couple by proxy in the Duomo. Unlike previous Medici fêtes these festivals, following the French pattern, were given by

44

RIGHT 144 Frans
Pourbus, *Marie de' Medici*

various people on different days. The Grand Duke's contribution was on the day of the marriage itself and took the form of an allegorical banquet in the Salone del Cinquecento of the Palazzo Vecchio. There was a buffet in the form of a *fleur de lys* and the legendary collection of Medici plate of gold, silver and other precious stones was on display. The banquet itself was a feast of compliment to the royal couple. One course was in the form of a winter landscape with a hunting scene, another dish was the lion of Florence, which opened to shower forth *fleurs de lys* and then to change into an eagle. There was a course on the theme of the labours of Hercules in compliment to the warrior bridegroom, and Marie had set before her an equestrian statue of her husband. Suddenly in the midst of the revelry two luminous clouds began to propel themselves above the feasters across the length of the Salone, while simultaneously a rainbow, the traditional emblem of peace, vaulted the table at which the young French Queen sat. In the clouds rode Juno drawn by peacocks and Minerva pulled by a unicorn. Juno began a contention with her sister goddess by complaining of her appearance at such peaceful nuptials. Minerva replied by gesturing to the rainbow and saying that she in fact brought love and peace. Together they celebrated the virtues of this martial king and ended with predictions of huge expansions of his empire even into the Orient. The dialogue had been written by Battista Guarino and the music was by Emilio de' Cavalieri.

Until the departure of the bride from Livorno fête succeeded fête. On 6 October Jacopo Corsi presented Jacopo Peri's *L'Euridice* with a libretto by Ottavio Rinuccini; on 7 October there was a *palio*; and on the eighth Riccardo Riccardi presented a tournament in his garden. There were rival bands of knights preceded by triumphal cars bearing Poliziano and Pindarus. The knights ran a *corso al saracino* and later Diana appeared to signal the beginning of the hunt. Peri's *L'Euridice* had six scenes, none of great complexity; Vittoria Archilei sang the name part and Peri himself sang Orfeo. The performance was a landmark in the history of the evolution of opera, being an expression of the Academy's aims of reviving Greek drama and antique singing. Although performed on the occasion of the marriage, there were no reasons especially to relate it in theme to the event.

Without doubt, however, the climax to the series of entertainments was that given by Gabbriel Chiabrera in the Gran Salone of the Uffizi. This was Caccini's *Il Rapimento di Cefalo*, with settings by Bernardo Buontalenti.

OVERLEAF
145 Bernardo
Buontalenti, *Design for the Prologue to 'Il Rapimento di Cefalo', 1600*

145

It was the architect's last great court spectacle and is recorded as having 'the most marvellous machines that until now have ever been seen in our times'. Caccini's *Il Rapimento di Cefalo* was again a triumph of the principles of the Academy for the composer had imitated the inflexions of speech, not losing the meaning amidst complex polyphonic music. The story was not in itself directly related to the marriage, although the official account cites it as an example of heroic virtue; but the opera as a whole was encompassed by a prologue and epilogue which incorporated the most staggering visual effects in celebration of the alliance. It opened with a mountain scene, in the centre of which rose a huge mount some 20 ells high covered with trees and bushes. On its summit stood the winged horse Pegasus, while below sat Apollo and the Muses. Down the hill there gradually descended the figure of Poetry, who advanced downstage and sang the praises of Henry IV and the new Queen, predicting, as had the goddesses at the banquet, a mighty destiny. The opera itself was full of astounding feats of engineering, but the greatest was yet to come. At the close the scene changed to a *gran teatro* in the Doric style with gilded columns and statues which architecturally continued the auditorium, so that the spectators seemed suddenly to find themselves incorporated within the *mise en scène*. Heroes stood on each side of the stage, while from below a vast machine slowly arose bearing Fame in a magnificent chariot, her wings extended and holding an olive branch and a trumpet. Beneath her sat eighteen ladies, representing towns over which the Grand Duke ruled, headed by the two cities of Florence and Siena, who sang the glories of the present Duke. While the chariot gradually ascended into the heavens the machine supporting it sank back below stage, allowing the ladies to alight and salute a huge scarlet lily, emblem of the city of Florence, which blossomed in the background and around which hovered the *palle* of the Medici family.

Marie de'Medici left Florence on 13 October and some days later sailed from Livorno in a squadron of ships furnished by her husband, her uncle, the Pope and the Order of St John. Accompanied by her aunt, the Duchess Christina, and her sister, the Duchess of Mantua, Marie landed at Marseilles on 9 November after a stormy journey. Travelling via Avignon to Lyon, into which she made a magnificent entry on 3 December, she at last married her husband on 10 December, the ceremony being yet again conducted by the papal legate, the Cardinal Aldobrandini. An English pamphlet sums up the whole transaction with tart accuracy: 'Thus much

146

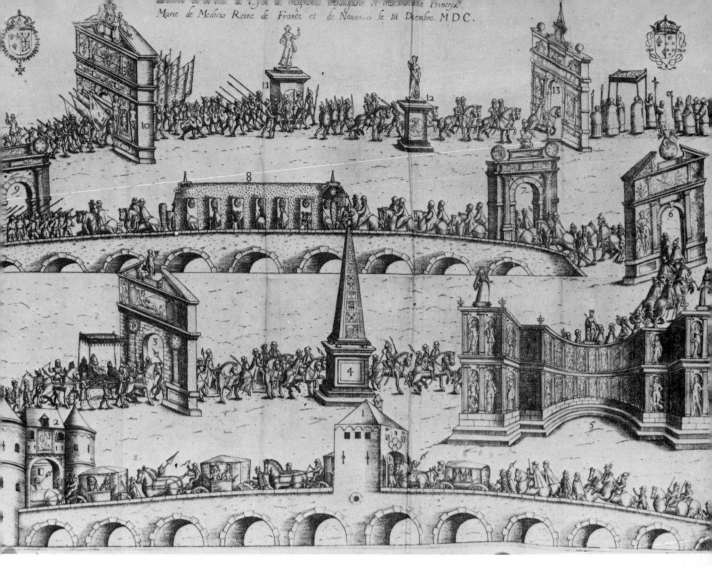

146 Marie de' Medici's Entry into Lyon, 1600

in breefe haue I written vnto you, of our Ladie the French Queenes entrie
into our citie of *Lyons*, whom I beseech God to preserue for vs, and shortly
to send her some issue, which is a thing that with all my heart I doe most
desire. ...'

This high-water mark of Medicean policy was not a success. Shortly after
relations between Henry and Ferdinand cooled, notably because the
French King refused to settle his debts and because he suddenly made
peace with the Grand Duke's enemy, the Duke of Savoy, ceding him
Saluzzo. This did not, however, mean a cessation of Ferdinand's liberal
conciliatory policies, but rather reflected the difficulties of his naval policy,
for which he needed the help of Spain in his war against the Turks and

147

148

corsairs, and his desire to receive from the new King, Philip III, the investiture of Siena, which was held from the Spanish Crown as a fief. His moderate nature and aversion to the excessive demands of Counter-Reformation popes found expression in his relations with James I of England and in his overt support of Venice in her famous quarrel with the Pope over the Servite, Paolo Sarpi. None the less his desire for peace with Spain was finally settled in 1608 when his son Cosimo married Maria Maddelena, daughter of the Emperor Rudolf II and sister of the Queen of Philip III of Spain.

The 1608 fêtes form an interesting epilogue to the reign of Ferdinand, who died a few months later. In the entry of the Habsburg Archduchess, Maria Maddelena, into Florence on 18 October 1608 any gestures towards heroic civic history were finally eliminated. This time the programme was that of absolutist rule. As usual the first arch was of the Tuscan order, but the two figures who dominated it were *Imperio di Terra* and *Imperio di Mare*, regal personages expressing the grand-ducal dominion over land and sea. References to the French royal house were omitted and the marriages to be recalled now were those of Alessandro de'Medici to Charles V's daughter, Margaret, and of Francesco to Joanna of Austria.

147 Sustermans,
Grand Duke Cosimo II

BELOW 148 *Maria Maddelena's Entry into Florence, 1608*

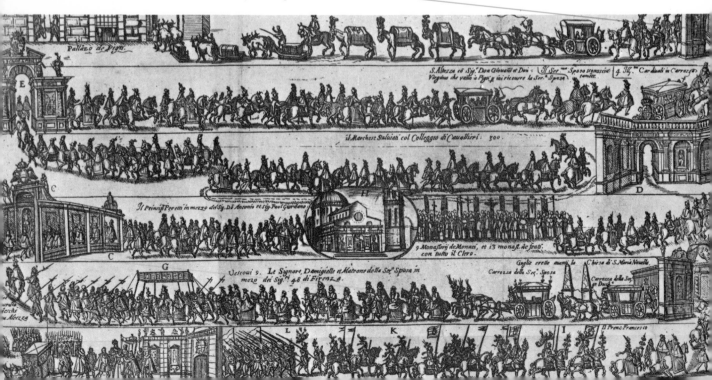

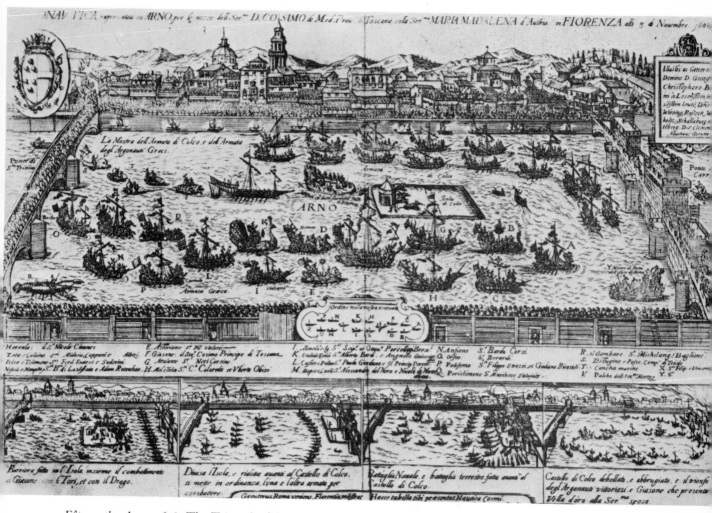

Fête on the Arno, 1608. The Triumph of the Argonauts (149–50): 149 View of the Arno

The decorations were relentlessly dynastic: an arch to glorify the house of Austria, a second in tribute to the bride's mother's family, the Wittelsbach of Bavaria, a third in honour of the house of Lorraine in salute to Duchess Christina and the inevitable apotheosis of the house of Medici. As in 1589 the fêtes spread over three weeks and were even more elaborate than those for Christina. There was the usual *corso al saracino*, a *calcio*, banquets and religious processions, but four stupendous spectacles surpassed all the other festivities. The first was a court ball interrupted from time to time by

150 *The Barge of Idmon and Mopsus*

Francesco Cini's *Notte d'Amore*, a series of sudden scenic wonders which took the dancers by surprise every so often and guided them through the passage of a single night in allegorical terms, with visions of Night with its fantastic dreams to Dawn. There was a horse ballet in emulation of the antique, the *Giostra dei Venti*, and a river fête, the *Argonautica*, with an obvious compliment to the bride in the quest for the Golden Fleece. This was staged on the Arno and the most extraordinary and exotic boats had been constructed to bear the knights to the combat.

149
150

But the climax was the intermezzi to adorn the play *Il Giudizio di Paride*, with settings by Buontalenti's successor, Giulio Parigi. Lacking the unity of those of 1589 they yet glorified the Medici and the new bride. The themes are ones – like the royal entry – concerned with the Medici. In the first a Palace of Fame made of mirror glass arose to receive the heroic ancestors of bride and groom. In the second the imperial eagle, with wings outspread, swept down from heaven bearing the maiden Astraea on its back, the Virgin who ushers in the Age of Gold on earth. Each of the virtues of the Golden Age, which was a fundamental Medicean myth, bore

151

152

206

The intermezzi of 1608 for 'Il Giudizio di Paride' (151–4):
151 *The first intermezzo. The Palace of Fame*

152 *The second intermezzo. The Return of Astraea*

154

153

one of the Medici *palle*. In honour of the Grand Duke's colonial enterprises the Florentine explorer Amerigo Vespucci sailed across the Indian
seas in a ship adorned with Florentine lilies and a lion, while the Cave of
Vulcan in a fiery Underworld furnace made armour for the young
Cosimo, whose valour was to be exercized against the barbarous corsairs.

The immense spectacle closed with a Prospero-like vision in which it
seemed as though in one composite image or diagram the Platonic 'ideas'
of Ferdinand's rule were realized. Through a trapdoor arose the goddess
of Peace enthroned before the Temple of Peace, in itself a building of
harmonious classical proportions. Grouped round Peace were the principles of Ferdinand's rule, an interesting assortment: Remembrance of Old
Friendship, Love of Country, Security, Faith, Concord, Abundance,
Innocence, Justice, Reverence, Natural and Civil Law. These were further
supported by fourteen priests, alluding to the piety of the Grand Duke's
rule, which had reached its climax in the negotiations for the transfer of the
Holy Sepulchre from Jerusalem to the Capella dei Principi in S. Lorenzo.
There was yet a further curious assemblage of abstractions of grand-ducal
government: Pleasure, Jest, Laughter, Forgetfulness of Injuries and Trade.
Four clouds then appeared carrying the Olympian anti-gods, Bellona,
Cybele, Pluto and Neptune, gods of violence and greed but also the means
to earthly power. Peace harnessed these forces by letting each serve Cosimo and his bride within their respective spheres, so through them the
virtues of Ferdinand's peaceful rule were extended to include war and
wealth, sea and land. These deities descended to stage level on their clouds
and dismounted to take up their places in tableaux depicting the terrestrial
and sub-terrestrial spheres now subservient to the Medici. The rejoicings
of earth were taken up to heaven, the clouds above revealing new har-

153 *The sixth intermezzo. The Temple of Peace*

monies culminating in a dance by Light Breezes, who floated in on two clouds from either side.

At the court of the grand dukes of Tuscany the theatre had developed into a machine for presenting the realm of Platonic ideas made apprehensible and visible. The grand duke and his audience of some three thousand were contemplating the divine ideas of the principles of which on earth the grand duke was the living embodiment. From these Neo-Platonic machines created by Vitruvian architect engineers stemmed the theatre of illusion.

OVERLEAF 154 *The fourth intermezzo.
The Ship of Amerigo Vespucci*

212

6 *A Royalist Arcadia*

CHARLES I

156
157

Charles I was nine when the Grand Duke Ferdinand died. Sixteen years later, in 1625, he was to marry the Duke's grand-daughter, Henrietta Maria, daughter of Marie de'Medici and Henry IV. This couple was to reign over the most brilliant and civilized court in Europe during the third decade of the seventeenth century until the mirage of peace and power they created vanished in a disastrous civil war. England, which had been on the fringes of Renaissance culture since the Reformation, suddenly became a focal point for everything of any importance that was happening within Europe in the arts. The King's agents scoured the Continent for paintings by the great artists of the Renaissance, especially those by the Venetian masters, Titian and Tintoretto. Among their greatest triumphs was the acquisition of the celebrated collection of the Duke of Mantua, including the famous Mantegna cartoons. To the court were attracted artists from abroad, the sculptors Francesco Fanelli and Hubert Le Sueur, the painters Daniel Mytens and Orazio Gentileschi, and above all Van Dyck. Even Rubens, the greatest exponent of the new Baroque style, visited Charles's court in 1629. But the presiding genius of this remarkable Renaissance was a man whose influence was seminal for the arts in England in whatever sphere he worked, the King's Surveyor of Works, Inigo Jones. Architect, painter, engineer, designer, connoisseur, collector, author, theoretician, he occupied a key place for nearly half a century at the courts of James I and Charles I. Together with Ben Jonson, Inigo Jones created that most distinctive manifestation of the art of festival at the Stuart court, the masque.

158

156 Van Dyck,
Henrietta Maria

The masque was essentially a composite form. This is difficult for us to grasp, for we assume the importance of the literary text because that alone remains today. But for a contemporary the primacy of what was sung or spoken did not necessarily follow. As in the case of the Florentine intermezzi it is impossible and pointless to disentangle the contributions of everyone: author, composer, designer, machinist and choreographer. However the history of the English court masque is dominated by two famous figures who created it as a form, Ben Jonson and Inigo Jones. *The Masque of Blackness* of 1605 is the first of the Stuart masques and *Salmacida Spolia* in 1640 the last. Until 1631, when they finally parted company, Jonson and Jones together produced these annual spectacles of State performed each Twelfth Night and Shrovetide. After their famous quarrel it is usual to regard the masque, as presented by Jones himself, with the assistance of various tame poets, as a decadent form in which what had

OPPOSITE 155 *Coelum Britannicum, 1634: Proscenium and Mountain scene*

157 Van Dyck, *Charles I on Horseback*

been essentially a poetic means of expression became overloaded with pointless visual spectacle. The quarrel of Jones and Jonson was not, in fact, as used always to be assumed, one of the visual versus the verbal. Their trouble lay in the very similarity and not the divergence of their views as to what made up the component parts of a court masque. Both of them printed their own definitions of these spectacles, seemingly different but in reality closely related. In 1631 Jonson wrote: '... all representations, especially those of this nature in court, public spectacles, either have been or ought to be the mirrors of man's life.' Jones the year after described them as 'nothing else but pictures with light and motion'.

158 Van Dyck, *Inigo Jones*

159

The great Caroline masques of the 1630s created by Inigo Jones are based, as one would expect, on sound Platonic doctrine. Jones in his own commentary to Aurelian Townshend's masque *Tempe Restored* elaborates his viewpoint when he states that he had designed the costume for Henrietta Maria 'so that corporeal beauty, consisting in symmetry, colour, and certain unexpressable graces, shining in the Queen's Majesty, may draw us to the contemplation of the beauty of the soul, unto which it hath an analogy'. Jonson's definition is really not so very different and has the same philosophical basis in Platonism. As the masque in his view is a 'mirror', such an object of necessity demands a spectator, and therefore this presupposes that the masque is essentially a visual form. For Jonson, as for Jones, the court is looking at its real self in the court masque, seeing itself as in a mirror. The climax of all these performances is when the masquers themselves are revealed, inhabitants of the realm of Platonic ideas, to link with the world of reality before them in the general dancing of the court, fusing idea and reality into one.

Jones's scenery was essentially the action of the masque which its dialogue, songs and dances elucidated and moralized, but first and foremost the masque was a statement made visually by means of engineering. Every stage picture he presented was a symbol composed of a composite series of hieroglyphs. To a Platonist such as Jones truths were best expressed in images, words occupying a lower place in the hierarchy of communication, being only the *name* of an *idea*, image or thing. The masques, therefore, belong directly to the Renaissance tradition of conceptualizing abstractions. Jones is a textbook Renaissance Platonist of no great originality in his own philosophical assumptions, which were derived from the standard books of reference by Renaissance architects and aesthetic theoreticians, who believed that it was images that *meant* and that words only *explained*. Jonson himself ironically belonged to the same tradition when he wrote: 'The conceits of the mind are Pictures of things, and the tongue is the Interpreter of those Pictures.' To Jones's direct and uncompromising Platonism one must add his discipleship of Serlio's assertion concerning the role of stage machinery as the means to evoke wonder in the minds of spectators and, above all, as a way of expressing the magnificence of monarchs.

To achieve his theatre of ideas Jones introduced to England for the first time perspective stage scenery, although it took the court many years to read this properly. Even in Oxford in 1636 there were still people unable to

159 Inigo Jones, *Design for Henrietta Maria as Divine Beauty in 'Tempe Restored', 1632*

understand the perspective stage scenery he had designed for the plays on the occasion of the King's visit. A bewildered observer described the side wings as being like desks or studies in a library. This inability to read stage pictures correctly reveals the importance of the collusion of the audience in understanding perspective, and the success of Jones's Platonic pictures depended on having an audience that would accept his thought and vision premises. In 1605, when Jones first used perspective in the first of the masques, Jonson's *Masque of Blackness*, all one courtier saw was a pageant car with a bevy of sea-monsters standing at one end of the hall, all fish and no sea, as he tartly remarked. It can be no coincidence either that perspective stage scenery was used for court performances only, and that its introduction in England coincides with the serious promotion of the theory of the Divine Right of Kings. Perspective made the ruler the emblematic and ethical centre of all court productions and emphasized the hierarchical gradations of court life.

The Stuart court masques, even more powerfully than the Florentine intermezzi, were Platonic 'ideas' made apprehensible by means of symbolic fables and miraculous resolutions. Courtiers were seen as heroes, kings became gods, actions were emblems, all of which demanded a viewer able to read the visual images unfolding before him. Occasionally he was helped by the spoken or sung dialogue; rarely there was a commentary published afterwards in which the hieroglyphs were unravelled for the vulgar. Even if the audience could not understand the frequently recondite allegories, one must never underestimate the considerable pleasure afforded a Renaissance audience at being in the presence of what Jonson once referred to as 'remov'd mysteries'. Inigo Jones's work for the Caroline court depended on an acceptance that seeing was believing, that the stage pictures he created had both a philosophical meaning and a moral force, and that in projecting illusions he was at the same time presenting a Platonic reality.

The collusion of the spectator is all important, for what he is really called upon to contemplate is mechanical marvels. The incessant use of mystic symbols, spells, incantations and miraculous visions of the celestial world, the glimpses of hell or the sudden arrival of spring in winter might seem magical, but they were magical only if the onlooker wished them to be. Rather he was admiring man's ability to create these illusions, to present visions of the physical world and then make them suddenly do the impossible. The masque in this sense, besides embodying Platonic truth,

160 Inigo Jones, *Design for a Forum in 'Albion's Triumph', 1632*

celebrates the power of the rational mind in controlling the physical
world. In it virtues are revealed, and the gods come down to earth, but the
ultimate in extraordinary revelations always happens at the climactic
moment when the audience itself is about to be included in the unfolding
fable by means of ritual dances. All the masques express the power of the
monarchy to bring harmony, the rich gifts of nature and the natural world
into obedience. All move from initial statements of disorder and cosmic
chaos towards revealing king and court abstracted in emblematic form as
gods and goddesses, heroes and heroines, sun and stars. Year after year the
exchequer poured money into these annual manifestations of harmonious
visions of Stuart rule. Unfortunately for Charles I the illusion of control
manifested in these spectacles was not to bring with it any actuality.

219

161 Inigo Jones, *Design for an Indian seascape in 'The Temple of Love', 1635*

The repertory of pictorial images needed to convey these set ideas was a very limited one: landscape, both wild and tame, the garden, the sea, the underworld, the storm, the villa, the palace, the street or piazza, classical ruins, the heavens and, very occasionally and within the tradition of the Italian theatre, re-creations of actual places. Every masque makes a visual progress from disorder to order or from order to disorder and back to a higher order again. For Jones there are therefore only ever two repertories of stage picture. The first are ones of nature untamed and unleashed: tempests, stormy seas, flaming hell scenes, impenetrable forests; the second those evoking earthly and cosmic harmony: elegant villas, piazzas and palaces in the classical style, the safety of a port, the beauty of a garden in full flower, or the virtues of heaven itself in the form of spectacular cloud apparitions and glimpses of stars and planets. For nearly four decades Inigo Jones was presenting the same visual argument on behalf of the Stuart kings.

Inigo Jones, it is well known, drew heavily on engravings of scenes created for intermezzi at the Florentine court, but there the coincidence ends, for the motives behind the visions evoked by the Medici court are very different from those for the court of England. The first scene in *Albion's Triumph* is derived from Parigi's *Temple of Peace* in the intermezzi for *Il Giudizio di Paride*, and the Indian shore in the *Temple of Love* is lifted

160, 153
161, 154

162 Inigo Jones, *Design for Oberon's Palace in 'Oberon', 1611. The palace was made up of two shutters which parted to reveal the interior.*

from *The Ship of Amerigo Vespucci* in the same series, but there the connection ends. Jones had travelled to Italy in 1613–15 in the train of the connoisseur and diplomat, Thomas Howard, Earl of Arundel, and studied closely, for instance, the Teatro Olimpico at Vicenza, but much of his stagecraft must have been self-invented, even if inspired by information from afar of the visual appearance of Florentine court spectacle. His early masques use a turning machine, a *machina versatilis* for surprise effects, but from about 1610 onwards he uses sliding shutters and side wings. These are used in Prince Henry's masque of *Oberon*, in which rock shutters slide back to reveal a fairy palace. By 1613, and probably from the very beginning, Jones had evolved an upper stage for heavenly tableaux, and in 1631 he introduced a fly gallery, allowing the front curtain to go up for the first time and deities to ascend out of sight. Cloud machines he continually elaborates and perfects over the years. In the early masques, for example, he developed the descent of a cloud bearing a chariot gently sloping downwards. By 1631 a cloud could descend to deposit a goddess in a throne on the stage and the cloud itself could be removed. During the 1630s, and again probably earlier, Jones made use of scenes of relieve, profiled cut-outs, sometimes three-dimensional, which were placed before the backcloth and revealed from time to time by parting the back-shutters. These were often used as set pieces to break the monotony of a

221

163 Inigo Jones, *Design for the Temple of Diana in 'Florimène', 1635. The temple was a scene of relieve made up of two or three layers of cut-outs placed in front of each other*

court play. The stage for the Stuart court masque was always a very shallow one, as the action took place mainly in the dancing area, which was reached by a combination of steps and slopes. From the evidence of the several hundred drawings that survive we know that Inigo Jones directly supervised the creation of the masques at all points, including the direction of the performers on stage. His drawings sometimes even show performers massed as part of the stage picture.

The masque is for the monarch and about the monarch. The more directly so in the reign of Charles I as the King himself danced the leading part in these annual spectacles of State. Both Jones and the King made every Stuart court masque a vehicle not only for Neo-Platonic doctrine, but for an exposition of the political theory of the Divine Right of Kings. To understand them we must be familiar with the treatise by the King's father on the rights and duties of a sacred king, the *Basilikon Doron*, which James I had composed for the edification of his elder son, Prince Henry. The central theme is not a complex one and can be summed up succinctly in the first two lines of the sonnet he wrote for the opening of the book:

> God gives not kings the stile of Gods in vaine:
> For on his throne his Scepter do they sway. ...

The King is the representative of God on earth and the greatest sin a subject can commit is to raise a hand in opposition. 'Therefore,' James instructed his son, 'you are little GOD to sit on his Throne, and rule over

167

other men.' The arguments on behalf of divine monarchy expounded in this book are more succinctly phrased in a speech James made to Parliament on 21 March 1609:

The state of Monarchy is the supremest thing upon earth: for Kings are not only God's lieutenants, and sit upon God's throne, but even by God himself they are called Gods. There be three principal similitudes that illustrate the state of Monarchy: one taken out of the word of God; and the two other out of the grounds of Policy and Philosophy. In the Scriptures Kings are called Gods, and so their power after a certain relation compared to the Divine power. Kings are compared to Fathers of families: for a King is trewly *Parens patriae*, the politique father of his people. And lastly, Kings are compared to the head of this Microcosm of the body of man.

Every masque devised by Inigo Jones is a visual realization of these principles to its courtly onlookers.

The artistic and scientific knowledge of Inigo Jones in his role as the Vitruvian architect-engineer was to set forth the politico-religious theories of the first two Stuart monarchs. In one of the few statements certainly from Jones's hand in a commentary to *Tempe Restored*, the masque for 1632, he makes one of the most extreme assertions concerning the nature of royalty to find voice during the period: 'In Heroic Virtue is figured the King's Majesty, who therein transcends as far as common man as they are above beasts he being the only prototype to all the kingdoms under his monarchy of religion, justice, and all the virtues joined together.' In this definition Jones fuses the Divine Right of Kings with early seventeenth-century developments within the *speculum principis* tradition. In tribute after tribute in the years of 'Personal Rule' the virtues and heroes of the past are not held up – as they had been in medieval and even humanistic mirrors – for imitation and emulation. The Divine Ruler does not need to model himself on examples from classical myth and antique history. In sharp contrast he surpasses them and it is his subjects who must study him as the living embodiment of the virtues. The task of Jones as the Vitruvian engineer was to translate into pictures with light and motion what one of the judges in the famous ship-money case involving John Hampden was to express as a legal principle. 'He is the first mover amongst these orbs of ours, and he is the circle of his circumference, and he is the centre of us all, wherein we all as the loins should meet. He is the soul of this body, whose proper act is to command.'

The Caroline masques all relate to the years of Charles's so-called 'Personal Rule', those eleven years between 1629 and 1640 in which he ruled without Parliament, a period subsequently branded by the opposition as the Eleven Years' Tyranny. In March 1629 Parliament was dissolved, never to reassemble until the unhappy months of 1640. At home, efforts were made to vivify and expand the antiquated Tudor administrative machinery. Charles found a brilliant statesman in Thomas Wentworth, Earl of Strafford, who was entrusted with establishing order in the north and in Ireland, and an efficient cleric in William Laud who, as successively Bishop of London and Archbishop of Canterbury, set about the radical overhaul of the strange patchwork that made up the Church of England. To understand the masques of Inigo Jones, which are so pure an expression of this decade, it is necessary to forget totally what happened after 1640 and to ignore, for the most part, Puritan opposition attitudes. It is essential to view these productions solely through the eyes of an optimistic King and his Surveyor of Works as they annually celebrated what they foolishly believed to be the triumphant rule of a monarch by Divine Right.

During the years of Personal Rule Jones *invented* the myths of the masques. This is quite specifically stated in *Tempe Restored*, where it is written that 'the subject and allegory of the masque with the descriptions and apparatus of the scenes, were invented by Inigo Jones', and only 'the verses were written by Mr. Townshend'. In the same way in the last of the masques he is openly credited with 'the invention, ornament, scenes and apparitions, with their descriptions'. Both these are making explicit what must have been the normal relationship that governed the creation of these spectacles between 1631 and 1640. Although Jones invented the subject matter of the masques, he must have done so in consultation with the King and Queen who acted in them.

Although Charles I ascended the throne in 1625, no great series of court entertainments began to be staged until the years of Personal Rule. By 1631, when the first, Ben Jonson's *Love's Triumph through Callipolis* and *Chloridia*, were staged, the mythology of the court was already fully developed. In these two masques the fundamental statements of Caroline mythology are forcefully made, and all the masques subsequent to them elaborate these preliminary statements. *Love's Triumph*, the King's masque, opens with an allegorical representation of the cleansing of the court. Anti-masquers as the distractions and perversions of love are banished from Callipolis, 'the city of beauty and goodness'. This is a pre-

164, 165
166

Love's Triumph thorough
Callipolis, 1631 (164–8):
164 A Whining Lover

165 A Fantastical Lover

166 A Melancholy Lover

face to the arrival of perfect love in the form of the King as Heroic Love
and his courtiers as other forms of exemplary devotion. These voyage to
pay tribute to the Queen, Henrietta Maria, who is celebrated as a terrestrial
manifestation of the Platonic Ideal of Beauty and Virtue. And here the
masque reveals itself as saturated in Neo-Platonism:

> To you that are by excellence a queen,
>   The top of beauty! but of such an air
> As only by the mind's eye may be seen
>   Your interwoven lines of good and fair.

Such a revelation of love cannot be achieved until the city has been puri-
fied, and so a chorus walks about bearing censers exorcizing the place.
Next the 'prospect of a sea appears', moving the court from the enclosed
world of the city and its buildings to vistas of the world of nature. And
across the sea float Charles and his train, a vision that would be read by
the court audience not only as an image of love, for Venus arose from the
waves, but as a political statement of British sea-power. All British monarchs from Elizabeth I onwards are celebrated as sovereigns of the seas.
Such a picture as the King bestriding the waves in triumph in Callipolis
evoked for onlookers innumerable previous images of maritime power

167

167 *Sketch for the sea triumph*

claimed by the Stuart kings. Indeed their rule was to founder on naval policy in the imposition of ship-money.

In a very precise analysis derived from Ficino's *Commentary on Plato's Symposium* Ben Jonson proceeds to define the relationship of the King to the Queen:

> For Love without his object soon is gone;
> Love must have answering love to look upon.
> To you, best judge, then, of perfection!
> The queen of what is wonder in the place!
> Pure object of heroic love alone!
> The centre of proportion, sweetness, grace!
> Deign to receive all lines of love in one,
> And by reflecting of them fill this space,
> Till it a circle of those glories prove
> Fit to be sought by beauty, found by Love.
> Where Love is mutual, still
> All things in order move;
> The circle of the will
> Is the true sphere of Love.

In these lines the Caroline court is cast as a circle in the midst of whose unexcepting orbit the Queen reigns as a Neo-Platonic love goddess over the passions. She is the 'centre of proportion' and in her the 'lines of love' meet. From her as the object of the King's devotion radiate 'glories' which fill this courtly circle, whose boundary is defined as the royal will. In this way Jonson defines the precepts of absolutist rule, casting the King as supreme sovereign over both intellect and will. The image of the circle, a geometric shape that allows no exceptions to its boundaries, is perhaps the most significant emblem of a new era.

Having established these principles Jones makes his Vitruvian machine mutate to demonstrate the fruits of such a policy. We move visually from earth to heaven, for the clouds above part to reveal 'Euclia, or a fair glory', who celebrates the creation of order and beauty within the cosmos while Neptune in the waves below summons from the deep a rock bearing the Muses. The Renaissance of the arts, the best-known aspect of the civilization of the court of Charles I, is a direct manifestation of this triumph of autocratic power. With these emblems of universal harmony and royal power giving birth to the arts set before the eyes of the onlookers, the masquers now join them in the ritual of the revels.

168 *Venus in her cloud machine*

At their close one final stage picture develops these images of earthly
royal policy into abstract Neo-Platonic ideas. The scene changes to a
garden, a vision of nature at its most tamed and cultivated. Once more the
clouds above part, this time to reveal the divine ideas of which Charles I
and Henrietta Maria seated beneath the State were terrestrial reflections –
Jupiter and Juno, the King and Queen of Heaven, attended by Hymen
and Genius, the gods of marriage and generation. They call upon Venus,
Queen of Love, who descends in a cloud which, when it reaches ground
level, is whisked away to reveal her enthroned. Love it is that links heaven
and earth, and the two Queens of Love, Henrietta Maria and Venus, con-

168

Chloridia, 1631 (169–73):
169 *A landscape*

template each other from opposite ends of the hall. The masque closes
with a simple allegory. Within this peaceful garden representing the State
of England grows a palm tree, the emblem of peace, bearing the British
crown, while round its trunk are entwined the lily and the rose.

   Chloridia, the Queen's Shrovetide masque, is complementary to *Love's
Triumph*. Its theme is the transformation of Chloris by the love of Zephyrus, the west wind, into Flora, goddess of Flowers. The curtain rises to reveal a pleasant landscape of hills and rivers to which this time Zephyrus
descends, calling upon Spring and asking that she execute Jove's bidding
to make the earth another heaven. This, Spring replies, has already been
accomplished by the flowers caused by 'yonder sun', gesturing towards
the King seated beneath his canopy. So in this masque we open with a vision of the King's peace, of heaven come down to earth, and move from it
through a myth that takes us first to hell, the anti-court, and then to a
vision of a higher harmony, the bower of Chloris. Cupid, we are told, is
in revolt and, forsaking his mother, has gone to hell, there exciting and
stirring up jealousies and other passions among the gods to 'raise a chaos of
calamity'. This is depicted in anti-masques that anatomize the ills of the
wrong sort of love. A dwarf postilion enters and satirizes what is in fact the
vicious underworld of the Stuart court, followed by a series of entrées in
the manner of the French *ballet de cour*, which move from the woes
wrought by Cupid – Jealousy, Disdain, Fear and Dissimulation – to the ills
caused by Zephyrus upsetting the cosmos with winds, tempests, lightning
and thunder. The evils are banished all of a sudden by the command of

170 *Zephyrus*

171 *A Dwarf Postilion*

Juno, goddess of marriage, who again, as in *Love's Triumph*, symbolized the ideal marriage of the King and Queen: '... the scene is changed into a delicious place figuring the bower of Chloris, wherein an arbour feigned of goldsmith's work, the ornament of which was borne up with terms of satyrs beautified with festoons, garlands and all sorts of fragrant flowers. Beyond all this in the sky afar off appeared a rainbow. ...'

The rainbow symbolizes peace, the King's peace, and the masquers led by Henrietta Maria represent the coming of Spring and the banishment of the disharmony of Winter. They celebrate their triumph in a dance, after which the heavens part to reveal Iris and Juno, who tell of the defeat of Cupid, who now sues for pardon. As in the case of *Love's Triumph*, this vision of nature tamed in the beauties of the garden, the handiwork of man civilizing wild nature, is an image of royal harmony. And as in *Love's Triumph* such benefits lead to a programme for the arts. 'Here out of the earth ariseth a hill, and on the top of it, a globe on which Fame is seen standing with trumpet in her hand; and on the hill are seated four persons, presenting Poetry, History, Architecture and Sculpture.' A life of virtue leads to heaven and the arts enable such noble acts to be immortalized. Fame slowly ascends into the clouds, leaving an earth transformed and rich with Juno's gifts: fountains, rivers, the Spring, the star flowers of the nymph Chloris. As Fame rises the hill sinks, the heavens close once more and the focus is shifted down to the dancing area below, where order and harmony are now expressed in the dance.

Every year for the next decade such statements on royal rule were to be

230

This deſigne I conceaue to bee fitt for the inuention and if it pleaſ hir ma:
to add or alter any thing J deſir to receaue hir ma:s comand and the
deſsigne againe by this bearer.   The colars allſo are in her ma:s
choiſ; but my oppinion is that ſeueral froſt coreenes mix with gould and
ſiluer will bee most propper.

172 *Henrietta Maria as Chloris*

made in the masques, which are the quintessential expressions of the mind of the Caroline court. These all, with one exception, propound the same principles of absolutist rule: power, they say, is love; opposition and rebellion are unleashed passions, both human and cosmological, the King is order, gentle, civilized, nature and peace. Only once, in Shirley's *Triumph of Peace*, offered to Charles by the Inns of Court to make amends for Puritan Prynne's implied attack on the Queen in his *Histriomastix*, do we hear a cautious voice of dissent to this confined arcadia so aptly described as a circle by Jonson. Not only did the anti-masques attack certain items in royal policy, but the ultimate triumph was a statement that the royal prerogative could not rule without law. This was the exception, for the court masques, as devised by Inigo Jones and Charles I through the 1630s, derived from a different but consistent philosophical position. They were primarily moving images whereby an audience apprehended moral and political truth. As Jones wrote in the commentary to one: 'Corporeal beauty consisting in symmetry, colour, and certain unexpressable graces … may draw us to the contemplation of the beauty of the soul unto which it hath an analogy.' The Caroline masque makes the onlooker apprehend the actual physical world round him by contemplating these artificial scenes as a series of images of divine and regal harmony.

Out of the eight masques staged until the last *Salmacida Spolia* in 1640, the greatest without doubt is Thomas Carew's *Coelum Britannicum*, performed on Tuesday, 18 February 1634, not only on account of the richness of its themes and its almost unbelievable mechanical marvels but also because Carew's text ranks as magnificent poetry. This masque was danced at the apogee of the years of Charles's Personal Rule. In the summer of 1633 he had travelled north to his kingdom of Scotland and was crowned king. Although the Calvinist clergy had been shocked by the splendour (or 'popery') of the Chapel Royal, the occasion was to all intents and purposes a triumph. The Scottish bishops had been summoned and charged to compile a version of the English *Book of Common Prayer* and in August of the same year William Laud was at last appointed Archbishop of Canterbury. Immediately measures were taken to prevent Puritans retaining their own ministers and chaplains, by insisting that those who were ordained must hold a benefice within the Established Church. Religious uniformity seemed therefore within grasp, while the judges' decision that year to uphold the royal prerogative over the imposition of ship-money seemed a victory for monarchical principles. All was, however, in reality little more than a postponement of disastrous troubles to come.

Coelum Britannicum is, therefore, a courtly celebration of the triumphs of Stuart absolutist rule. The curtain rises on a scene of the classical ruins of a great city of the Romans or Ancient Britons. Mercury descends and, going up to the Queen, announces Jove's intention of transforming his realm of heaven into such a pattern of the virtues as was the English court:

> Your exemplar life
> Hath not alone transfused a zealous heat
> Of imitation through your virtuous court,
> By whose bright blaze your Palace is become
> The envied pattern of this underworld,
> But th' aspiring flame hath kindled heaven. …

The speech introduces us immediately to a fundamental thought assump-

174

tion of the years of Charles's Rule, that is, that the court was a model of the
virtues. Its success is such that Jove now wishes to re-create heaven in
imitation of this earthly Olympus. Charles and Henrietta Maria followed
the precepts of James I in his *Basilikon Doron* in making their court 'a
patterne of godlinesse and all honest virtues'. Lucy Hutchinson, looking
back several years later, describes the ethos of the new court exactly in the
memoirs of her husband:

The face of the court was much changed in the change of the King, for King

Coelum Britannicum, 1634
(174–9):
174 *A ruined city*

234

Charles was temperate, chaste, and serious; so that the fools and bawds, mimics and catamites, of the former court, grew out of fashion; and the nobility and courtiers, who did not quite abandon their debaucheries, yet so reverenced the king as to retire into corners to practise them.

Momus, god of satire, now makes his entrance, and Jove's plans for the reformation of the heavens are related in a parody of those achieved by Charles I. The purge is narrated before a vast figure of Atlas bearing up the starry sphere of heaven on which all the constellations are placed. It

175

235

opens with Jove himself admitting to his own reformation of character in renouncing 'all lascivious extravagances and riotous enormities of his forepast licentious life'. Then comes a list of topical reforms:

Monopolies are called in, sophistication of wares punished, and rates imposed on commodities. Injunctions are gone out to the nectar brewers for the purging of a heavenly beverage of a narcotic weed which hath rendered the Ideas confused in the divine intellects, and reducing it to the composition used in Saturn's reign. Edicts are made for the restoring of decayed housekeeping, prohibiting the repair of families, to the metropolis. ... Bacchus hath commanded all taverns to be shut, and no liquor drawn after ten at night.

Momus is rehearsing to the Whitehall audience a parody of royal edicts issued early in 1634 forbidding the misrepresentation or adulteration of goods: vintners were forbidden to sell tobacco (the heavenly beverage of a narcotic weed); inns were ordered to cease cooking game birds, which was curiously believed to be a way of making London life less attractive to gentlemen, thus encouraging their return to the labours of the countryside.

These reforms are matched by a new code of sexual morality and the practice of marital fidelity: 'Cupid must go no more so scandalously naked, but it is enjoined to make him breeches, though of his mother's petticoats. Ganymede is forbidden the bedchamber, and must only minister in public. The gods must keep no pages, nor grooms of their chamber, under the age of 25, and those provided of a competent stock of beard.' So in allegorical terms Momus describes what Lucy Hutchinson relates as a historical fact, the re-establishment of sexual decency at court and the exile of those who failed to conform, survivals from the depraved reign of the King's father. The virtues of marriage are then exalted. Both Venus and Jupiter, we are told, have returned to their marriage partners and now indulge in conjugal affection. Jupiter indeed 'to eternize the memory of that great example of matrimonial union which he derives from hence, hath on his bedchamber door and ceiling fretted in stars with capital letters, engraven the inscription of CARLO MARIA'. So the masque follows the pattern of all others in establishing the perfection of the union of the King and Queen as an example to all, both in their roles as knight and romantic heroine, and as ideal husband and wife.

There then followed a series of anti-masques in which the hideous vices embodied in the licentious Ovidian constellations are expelled in turn from the firmament. One by one the star formations were extinguished from the celestial sphere on stage until it was left in total darkness. Before, however, the new Olympus of the Stuart court can give it new, more virtuous, light, various other claimants come forward: Plutus, god of riches; Poenia or Poverty; Fortune and Pleasure. All these are spurned:

> ... we advance
> Such virtues only as admit excess,
> Brave bounteous acts, regal magnificence,
> All-seeing prudence, magnanimity
> That knows no bound, and that heroic virtue
> For which antiquity hath left no name,
> But patterns only, such as Hercules,
> Archilles, Theseus.

At this point the story takes up the opening pictorial statement of the masque, the ancient British ruins, for the Caroline court is the reviver of these long vanished glories, the bringers to perfection of a historical process. They are therefore, at this juncture, bidden to view this less perfect British society, the 'rude, and old abiders here', forerunners of the civilization of new, reunited Britain: '... a new scene appears of mountains, whose eminent height exceed the clouds, which pass beneath them; the lower parts are wild and woody: out of this place comes forth a more grave antimasque of Picts, the national inhabitants of this isle, ancient Scots and Irish: these dance a pyrrica or martial dance.' To the audience these recalled the Britain of antiquity, a preface to a vision of the Stuart imperial *renovatio* which, in the figure of the person of James VI of Scotland and I of England, had reunited the three kingdoms once more into their ancient unity. And now, at this moment, Jones introduces his most spectacular machine to celebrate that most frequent theme of Stuart panegyric, the creation of the Empire of Great Britain. Since the proclamation of 1604 masques, poems, medals, eulogies and inscriptions had sung of the benefits showered on this island by the Stuart resumption of the imperial diadem. The crown as reassumed for this empire was not a new creation but a return to ancient purity, to a time when this island had been ruled by the King's ancestors, the Trojan King Brutus and his descendants. The Vitruvian machine now gave spectacular expression to this achievement of Stuart politics:

> ... there began to arise out of the earth the top of a hill, which by little and little grew to be a huge mountain, that covered all the scene; the underpart of this was wild and craggy, and above somewhat more pleasant and flourishing; about the

55

237

176 *Torchbearer*   177 *Charles I as a British Hero*

middle part of this mountain were seated the three kingdoms of England, Scotland and Ireland, all richly attired in regal habits, appropriated to the several nations, with crowns on their heads, and each of them bearing the ancient arms of the kingdoms they represented.

At the top sat the Genius of Great Britain with a cornucopia filled with corn and fruits, symbolizing the abundance and peace of Charles's rule. A chorus is summoned of Rivers and Druids, ancient British priests, who spy the darkened sphere but who find a new radiant light to replace it in the virtuous beams shed by the Queen. Now the time has come, after purging followed by the vision of a less perfect British civilization, to realize and figure forth the glories of this present age, its fulfilment in Charles I and twelve other great lords who enter as British Worthies, epitomizing a new heroic age of Great Britain reborn. These descend and dance their entry, after which yet again the great machine evokes new wonders and develops in emblematic form the ideals of this new culture:

> The dance being past, there appears in the further part of the heaven coming down a pleasant cloud, bright and transparent, which coming softly downwards before the upper part of the mountain, embraceth the genius, but so as through it all his body is seen; and then rising again with a gentle motion bears up the genius of the three kingdoms, and being past the airy region, pierceth the heavens, and

238

178 *A Princely Villa*

is no more seen. At that instant the rock with the three kingdoms on it sinks, and is hidden in the earth.

This staggering feat by which Jones enraptured his audience with wonder 'gave great cause of admiration' in the same way as Buontalenti's amazing feats of engineering left members of the Medici court *stupiti*.

Genius during her ascent proclaims that these British Worthies shall adorn the starry firmament, but the kingdoms below beg that they should be allowed to remain and grace the earth. Genius replies that it is not themselves but their fame alone that will kindle new constellations in the heavens. Once more the scene changes, moving from fastnesses of mountains and wild scenery to a glimpse of the new civilization of the Caroline court:

178

    … the nearest part showing a delicious garden with several walks and parterres set round with low trees, and on the sides against these walks were fountains and grots, and in the furthest part a palace from whence went high walks upon arches, and above them open terraces planted with cypress trees, and all this together was composed of such ornaments as might express a princely villa.

Nature controlled in the beauties of a Renaissance garden; a vision of a palace built in the new classical style. This is the world of the new gardens, by Isaac de Caus at Wilton or the Queen's privy garden at Somerset

239

179 *The Great Cloud*

House, allied to palace building of a type the King longed to realize. At this point, in a setting directly expressing the ideals of the present age of the benefits of the civilized life made possible by the beneficent rule and example of Charles I, the masquers united with the audience in the revels.

There was yet one more spectacle to come. At the close of the revels, which lasted a great part of the night, Jones takes this world of the specific to that of the abstract. He conjures up a diagram of the Platonic ideas upon which Charles I based his government:

179

> ... for conclusion to this masque there appears coming forth from one of the sides, as moving by a gentle wind, a great cloud, which arriving at the middle of the heaven, stayeth; this was of several colours, and so great that it covered the whole scene. Out of the further part of the heaven begins to break forth two other clouds, differing in colour and shape; and being fully discovered, there appeared sitting in one of them Religion, Truth, and Wisdom. ... In the other cloud sat Concord, Government, and Reputation. ... These being come down in an equal distance to the middle part of the air, the great cloud began to break open, out of which struck beams of light; in the midst suspended in the air, sat Eternity on a globe. ...

The identification of these emanations of the royal mind with government. policy was emphasized in the distant view of one of the royal palaces, Windsor Castle. Round Eternity shone fifteen stars, one larger than the rest figuring the King. In this final scene came a last compliment, for Windsor Castle was that seat of revived Caroline chivalry, the Order of the Garter, on the reorganization of whose rites and ceremonies Charles lavished much care and attention.

A study in depth of any of the Caroline masques reveals that no other form gives such a penetrating glimpse into the mind of Charles I. The seriousness and the passionate belief in their remedial efficacy is reflected above all in the closing masques of the reign. They offer overt evidence of the confidence the King and Inigo Jones placed in the effect of these spectacles in staving off the oncoming tide of disaster. In 1635 the famous Rubens canvases were inserted into the ceiling of the Whitehall Banqueting House. No longer could this be used as the court's *salle des fêtes* for fear of the heat of the blazing torches damaging the paintings. They in themselves provided in permanent form a pattern of Neo-Platonic ideas hovering above the heads of the court below, just as the masques did in a more ephemeral way. But late in 1637 a masquing room had to be built with all speed. The King had something to say and the masque was his mouthpiece. Sir William Davenant's *Britannia Triumphans* was performed during the ship-money trial and it directly apotheosizes the righteousness of the King's naval policy and ends with a vision of the ship-money fleet. Charles as Britannocles, the glory of the western world, is again exhibited as the Platonic perfection of kingship.

But alas, by 1638 example of virtue alone was no longer sufficient power to control an increasingly unruly opposition. The thought tenets of the masque world were beginning to wear thin. By 1640, the year of the last of the masques, Davenant's *Salmacida Spolia*, they were almost threadbare. With an empty exchequer and an appalling political situation, Charles still practised the masque daily, his faith in the efficacy of such spectacles even at that late hour still apparently not shattered. But in this final masque he is no longer cast as triumphant. He is Philogenes, the Platonic king, doomed to reign in adverse times. His power is endurance and his chief virtue patience:

> O who but he could thus endure
> To Live and govern in a sullen age,
> When it is harder far to cure
> The people's folly than resist their rage.

It is no longer possible for Inigo Jones to reveal to men the Good and expect them tamely to follow it. The final scene is perhaps the most eloquent and touching of all those devised for the Stuart masques. It is a Vitruvian apotheosis, celebrating through architecture and engineering a glory that reality was shortly to deny the Stuart monarchy:

180

    ... the scene was changed into magnificent buildings composed of several selected pieces of architecture. In the furthest part was a bridge over a river, where many people, coaches, horses, and such like, were seen to pass to and fro. Beyond this on the shore were buildings in prospective, which shooting far from the eye showed as the suburbs of a great city.

241

180 John Webb after Inigo Jones, *The last scene of 'Salmacida Spolia', 1640*

From the highest part of the heavens came forth a cloud far in the scene, in which were eight persons richly attired representing the spheres. This joining with two other clouds which appeared at that instant full of music, covered all the upper part of the scene; and at that instant, beyond all these, a heaven opened full of deities; which celestial prospect, with the chorus below, filled all the whole scene with apparitions and harmony.

Everything Jones believed in was woven together in this single emblematic stage scene: the cosmic harmony of the universe is overtly linked with the classical architecture below, which, built according to Renaissance canons, reflected the harmony of the heavens. All symbolized the harmony of the King's love for the Queen and their mutual love for their people. The masque, Jones wrote, was 'the noblest and most ingenious that hath been done here in that kind'. That the audience viewed its message with apprehension may be gathered from Jones's remark that it 'was generally approved of, especially by all strangers'. Or as one member of the court put it even more succinctly: 'I was wise enough not to attend', thereby testifying less to the dangerous efficacy of apparitions and harmony than to their total irrelevance. This observation struck the death-knell of the power of the art of Inigo Jones. In the end it was to strike the death-knell of the art of the Renaissance court spectacle.

181 *Maquette for the ballet 'La Prosperité des Armes de France', 1641*

7 *Epilogue: Princely Magnificence*

By the third decade of the seventeenth century the themes of the Renaissance court fête had moved from a contemplation of cosmic harmony and its reflection in the State to a contemplation of the monarch as the genesis of that earthly and heavenly harmony. In short, we have arrived in the period of absolutism. The ballets performed by Louis XIII's court, the masques in which Charles I danced or the intermezzi unravelled for the eyes of the later Medici grand dukes gradually cease to represent an aspiration towards political order and become an expression of its actual fulfilment in the prince. This can be taken as perhaps the most significant thought line dividing the Renaissance from the Baroque festival.

All over Europe we can trace this happening as we progress into the opening decades of the seventeenth century. In 1581, in the *Balet Comique de la Reyne*, Henry III of France wages a war in allegorical terms with the vices and evils besetting his kingdom and is aided by harmonious and celestial powers to victory. In 1641 *Le Ballet de la Prosperité des Armes de France* opens with Harmony peacefully hovering in a cloud. The ballet thus begins with an accomplished fact, the good and beneficent rule of Louis XIII and his great minister, Cardinal Richelieu. Subsequently there follows a hell vision, representing vanquished opposition to royalist policies, and the ballet ends with Olympus descending to praise the figure of the King under the guise of the Gallic Hercules. No less forcefully can this shift be traced in the French royal entry. Already, under Henry IV, they had begun to become obsessed with the king as the Messianic ruler, saving the kingdom from the horrors of civil war, but by 1622 his son, Louis XIII, entered Avignon through a series of street decorations that were a progression through abstract emanations of the royal mind. The procession passed through the royal virtues, the Gateway of Felicity, the Trophy of Wisdom, the Fountain of Justice and the Theatre of Fortitude and Piety towards the Palace of Glory. Six years later the idea is restated with even greater emphasis in Louis's entry into Paris after the surrender of La Rochelle. There was once again a progression through his virtues, this time towards an arch dedicated to the eternity of the King's glory, the reward of having reduced the Huguenot stronghold, *'l'ouvrage le plus cyclopéen … des temps modernes'*.★ This is the imagery of absolutism, paralleled by development within contemporary political theory. We have arrived at the thought premises of the festivals of Louis XIV.

★ '… the most Cyclopaean work … of the modern era.'

Louis XIII's Entry into Paris, 1629 (182–5):
182 *The King's Clemency*

183 *The King's Prudence*

In Elizabethan England knights had come in disguise to honour the Queen as a romantic heroine, as the preserver and bringer of peace and plenty to her people. When Elizabeth I visited Lord Hertford in 1591 at Elvetham she was met by the Graces and the Hours, who walked before her celebrating the second Spring that her presence engendered. The power of her virtues was such that three years later in the Gray's Inn court masque she could draw the lodestone itself and rescue the Knights of the Adamantine Rock. But the patterns of her powers were limited. She could restore sight, reconcile warring parties, banish spells and charms, release the imprisoned, cause country folk to revel in her presence or bring the peaceful pastoral of the Golden Age. These are fanciful extensions of a political reality, that Elizabeth of England, through her politic govern-ment, had given her people wise and just rule. At no point is the direct and uncompromising equation made by her successors indulged in. Charles I does not bring peace, he *is* peace. Subjects pay homage to the King not because his good rule has brought peace but because he is the abstract personification of it on earth. The Caroline court is not only a reflection of the virtues of Olympus, it is so marvellous and miraculous that heaven itself must be purged and model itself on this earthly court. So runs, as we have seen, the argument of Carew's great spectacle *Coelum Britannicum*. This epitomizes the great and fundamental shift in attitude to the monarch. By the closing years of the third decade of the seventeenth century the relentless glorification typical of Tudor propaganda has

246

184 *The King's Fame*

185 *The King's Piety*

changed into the concrete deification promoted by the Stuart dynasty.

Revamped medieval romance, the imagery of sacred empire, of Christian and classical mythology provide the absolutist monarch with a repertory universally understood to promote his rule. In spite of the rise of scientific thought and method by the middle of the seventeenth century, the vitality of such material was remarkable, particularly when one realizes that it relied for its 'power' on the acceptance of a Neo-Platonic pattern of philosophical thought and on a universe pre-Copernican in its structure. The Renaissance court festival handed on to the Baroque court a set repertory of themes that continued to be acted out with increasing monotony throughout the seventeenth and into the early eighteenth century. By the middle of the seventeenth century court fêtes have become a codified piece of apparatus related to the pattern of life of the Baroque prince. The heroic days of the sixteenth century, when they seemed to touch so closely the living tensions and realities of the hour, had gone for ever.

For the modern reader the central thought tenet that motivated Renaissance court fêtes is the least interesting one. We can see them in retrospect for what they were: extravagant assertions of a mirage of power. They retain their fascination 350 years later only because through this alliance of art and power arose our modern opera and ballet and the theatre of illusion. In this century festivals have been studied seriously mostly as a curious ancestor of theatre, but they are in reality much more a branch of

247

186 *Sea monster in Francis, Duke of Anjou's Entry into Antwerp, 1582*

political history and thought. Within that area, for the most part, they are concerned with what might have been and, as such, are mostly despised by the academic historian as serious evidence. And yet these ephemera tell us so much of the hopes and aspirations of the hour, albeit what they say often seems to us now absurd and irrelevant or their arguments sometimes appear ridiculous. The alliance of two Troy-descended princes such as Charles IX and Elizabeth of Austria presaged to some in 1571 visions of a universal empire by their heir. To us the belief that the union of two descendants of Charlemagne would produce such a world emperor is absurd, but it was not at the time. To us it is pathetic to watch the foolish

186

Duke of Anjou, Catherine de'Medici's youngest son, received with splendour into Antwerp in 1582 as a reincarnated Duke of Burgundy. But to those present at the time, wearied by years of terrible civil war and

187

religious persecution, this is precisely what they hoped he would be. So, too, we think there is something faintly comic in the young Elector Palatine circling round the tiltyard at Heidelberg in a ship disguised as Jason having brought home the Golden Fleece. But in 1613 that Golden Fleece was the Princess Elizabeth of England and in this way the young Frederick had made a natural statement within the language of the time of his achievement, a marriage into the house of Stuart. So it is that as long as there is room left in the study of history for the consideration of what might have been, there will be a place for the evocation of the splendour of Renaissance spectacle and illusion.

187 *Frederick V, Elector Palatine as Jason. Tournament at Heidelberg to celebrate his marriage to the Princess Elizabeth, 1613*

Information Index

Listed here are some of the most important books and articles which have added substantially to our understanding of the motives and meaning of the Renaissance court fête. No attempt has been made to include all the original and secondary sources that have been consulted in the compilation of this book. The list below is rather a guide into the subject for those who wish to follow the theme in more depth and at greater length. Most contain extensive bibliographies within their sphere of interest.

GENERAL

PER BJURSTRÖM, *Giacomo Torelli and Baroque Stage Design* (Stockholm 1961).
Important book on the origin and development of the perspective stage set with
a catalogue of Torelli's work.

JAKOB BURCKHARDT, *The Civilisation of the Italian Renaissance*.
The fundamental text on the idea of the Renaissance festival. Still illuminating,
though dated.

R. CLEPHAN, *The Tournament, its periods and phases* (London 1919).
Technical account of one of the fundamental festival forms but of little value for
details on dramatic elaboration and decoration.

Enciclopedia dello Spettaculo (Rome 1954–66).
Profusely illustrated with good introductory articles on a number of aspects of the
art of festival; valuable recent bibliographies.

GEORGE R. KERNODLE, 'Renaissance Artists in the Service of the People. Political
Tableaux and Street Theaters in France, Flanders, and England', *Art Bulletin*,
XXV (1943), pp. 59–64.
Insubstantial article on an important theme.

EMILE MAGNE, *Les Fêtes en Europe au XVIIe Siècle* (Paris 1930).
General, profusely illustrated, survey almost exclusively of French festivals.
Dated text.

GABRIEL MOURREY, *Les Fêtes françaises* (Paris 1930).
Dated, lavishly illustrated, survey of French festivals from the late Middle Ages
to Napoleon.

WALTER J. ONG, 'From Allegory to Diagram in the Renaissance Mind: A Study
in the Significance of the Allegorical Tableau', *Journal of Aesthetics and Art
Criticism*, XVII (1959), pp. 423–40.
Discussion of an idea important for the understanding of Renaissance festivals.

ROBERT WITHINGTON, *English Pageantry. An Historical Outline* (Cambridge,
Mass. 1918).
Dated but still valuable survey of the whole field of English pageantry, both civic
and courtly.

THE ROYAL ENTRY (See also under the other headings.)

SYDNEY ANGLO, 'The London Pageants for the Reception of Katherine of Aragon: November 1501', *Journal of the Warburg and Courtauld Institutes*, XXVI (1963), pp. 53–89.
Important analysis of the extremely erudite programme devised for the arrival of Katherine of Aragon prior to her marriage to Prince Arthur.

CHARLES READ BASKERVILL (ed.), *Pierre Gringoire's Pageants for the Entry of Mary Tudor into Paris* (Chicago 1934).
Good example of a late medieval entry with illuminations of the pageants.

JOSÈPH CHARTROU, *Les Entrées Solennelles et Triomphales à la Renaissance, 1484–1551* (Paris 1928).
The standard account of the importation of the *à l'antique* triumph from Italy into France. Dated but still valuable.

Entrées Royales et Fêtes Populaires à Lyon du XVe au XVIIIe Siècles, Bibliothèque de la Ville de Lyon (12 June–12 July 1970).
Valuable exhibition catalogue listing all the sources available for the study of royal entries into Lyon from 1389 (Charles VI) to 1658 (Louis XIV).

BERNARD GUENÉE and FRANÇOISE LEHOUX, *Les Entrées Royales Françaises de 1328 à 1515*, Sources d'Histoire Mediévale, Institut de Récherche et d'Histoire des Textes, CNRS (Paris 1968).
Calendar of sources for medieval French royal entries.

ANTOINETTE HUON, 'Le Thème du Prince dans les Entrées Parisiennes au XVIe Siècle', in *Les Fêtes de la Renaissance*, ed. J. Jacquot, CNRS (Paris 1956), pp. 21–30.
The imagery of State entries as a reflection of Renaissance humanist concepts of the Prince.

GEORGE KUBLER, 'Archiducal Flanders and the *joyeuse entrée* of Philip III in 1619', *Koninklijk Museum voor Schöne Kunsten, Jaarboek* (1970), pp. 157–211.
Analysis of the entry of Philip III into Lisbon and the influence upon it of Low Countries' entries.

JOHN LANDWEHR, *Splendid Ceremonies. State Entries and Royal Funerals in the Low Countries 1515–1791* (Leiden 1971).
Useful bibliography and illustrations but no analytical text.

G. A. MARSDEN, 'Entrées et Fêtes Espagnoles au XVIe Siècle', in *Les Fêtes de la Renaissance*, ed. J.Jacquot, II, CNRS (1960), *Fêtes et Cérémonies au Temps de Charles Quint*, pp. 389–411.
Survey of the Spanish royal entry, tracing the gradual introduction of Renaissance forms and imagery.

MARGARET MCGOWAN, 'Form and Themes in Henry II's Entry into Rouen', *Renaissance Drama*, new series, I (1968), pp. 199–251.
Important article examining Henry II's entry in all its many and complex aspects.

PER PALME, 'Ut Architectura Poesis', *Acta Universitatis Upsaliensis*, in *Figura*, new series, I, pp. 95–107.
Important article establishing the application of Renaissance theories concerning architectural harmonic proportion to the arches for James I's entry into London in 1604.

ROBERT PAYNE, *The Roman Triumph* (London 1962).
Contains a useful survey in English of the traditions of the Roman imperial triumph, with a section on its revival during the Renaissance.

I. VON ROEDER-BAUMBACH and H. G. EVERS, *Versieringen bij Blijde Inkomsten gebruikt inde Zuidelijke Nederlanden gedurende de 16de en 17de eeuw* (Antwerp 1943).
Valuable, profusely illustrated survey of the royal entry in the southern Low Countries from Charles V in 1515 to the Cardinal Infant Ferdinand in 1635.

V. L. SAULNIER, 'Sebillet, du Bellay, Ronsard. L'Entrée de Henri II à Paris et la Révolution Poètique de 1550', in *Les Fêtes de la Renaissance*, ed. J. Jacquot, CNRS (Paris 1956), pp. 31–59.
Discusses the impact of avant-garde humanism on the Paris entry of 1550.

RÉNÉ SCHNEIDER, 'Le Thème du Triomphe dans les Entrées Solennelles en France à la Renaissance', *Gazette des Beaux-Arts*, IX (1913), pp. 85–106.
Still useful pioneering article on the transformation of the medieval French royal entry into an *à l'antique* triumph.

CARL VAN DE VELDE and HANS VLIEGHE, *Stadsvier ingen te Gent in 1635 voor de Blijde Intrede van Kardinal-Infant*, Oudheidkundig Museum Abdijvan de Blijloke (Ghent 1969).
Exhibition on the entry of the Cardinal Infant Ferdinand into Ghent in 1635. Contains all the documentation, including surviving paintings actually used in the street decorations.

M. VARCHAWSKAYA, 'Certains traits particuliers de la décoration d'Anvers par Rubens pour l'Entrée triomphale de l'Infant-Cardinal Ferdinand en 1635', *Bulletin des Musées Royaux des Beaux-Arts de Belgique* (1967), pp. 269–94.
Valuable article on the significance of Rubens's work for the entry of 1635 for the Cardinal Infant Ferdinand into Antwerp, with illustrations of the artist's sketches.

E. M. VETTER, 'Der Einzug Philipps III in Lissabon 1619', *Spanische Forschungen der Görresgesellschaft*, 19 (1962), pp. 187–263.
Long analysis of the street decorations for Philip III's entry into Lisbon in 1619.

BALLET

AGNE BEIJER, 'La Naissance de la Paix. Ballet de cour de Réné Descartes', in *Lieu théâtral à la Renaissance*, ed. J. Jacquot, CNRS (Paris 1964), pp. 409–22.
Interesting account of the introduction of *Ballet de cour* into Sweden and Descartes's ballet to celebrate the Treaty of Westphalia in 1648.

MARIE-FRANÇOISE CHRISTOUT, *Le Ballet de Cour de Louis XIV 1643–1672*, *Vie Musicale en France sous les Rois Bourbons*, 12, CNRS (Paris 1967).
Valuable survey, though less comprehensive than Miss McGowan's book listed below.

PAUL LACROIX, *Ballet et Mascarades de tour de Henri III à Louis XIV*, Geneva, 1868.
Important collection of texts for the ballets.

MARGARET MCGOWAN, *L'Art du Ballet de Cour en France 1581–1643*, CNRS (Paris 1963).
The most important survey and analysis of the evolution of the art of *ballet de cour*. There is a complete calendar and bibliography of ballets and the book is valuable for its insight into nearly every attitude governing the Renaissance court fête.

HENRY PRUNIÈRES, *Le Ballet de Cour en France avant Benserade et Lully* (Paris 1914).
Dated though still eminently readable account of the evolution of *ballet de cour*.

FESTIVALS FOR THE EMPEROR CHARLES V

SYDNEY ANGLO, 'Le Camp du Drap d'Or et les Entrevues d'Henri VIII et de Charles Quint', in *Les Fêtes de la Renaissance*, ed. J. Jacquot, II, CNRS (1960), *Fêtes et Cérémonies au Temps de Charles Quint*, pp. 113–34.

SYDNEY ANGLO, 'The Imperial Alliance and the Entry of the Emperor Charles V into London: June 1522', *The Guildhall Miscellany*, II, 4 (1962), pp. 131–55.
Account of the street pageants to welcome Charles V and celebrate the imperial alliance of 1522.

ANDRÉ CHASTEL, 'Les Entrées de Charles Quint en Italie', in *Les Fêtes de la Renaissance*, ed. J. Jacquot, œœ, CNRS (1960), *Fêtes et Cérémonies au Temps de Charles Quint*, pp. 197–206.
Account of the Emperor Charles V's Italian progresses in 1530 and 1535–6.

A. CORBET, 'L'Entrée du Prince Philippe à Anvers en 1549', in *Les Fêtes de la Renaissance*, ed. J. Jacquot, II, CNRS (Paris 1960), *Fêtes et Cérémonies au Temps de Charles Quint*, pp. 00–00.
Account of the entry of 1549.

DANIEL DEVOTO, 'Folklore et Politique en Château Ténébreux', in *Les Fêtes de la Renaissance*, ed. J. Jacquot, II, CNRS (1960), *Fêtes et Cérémonies au Temps de Charles Quint*, pp. 311–28.
Important article on the great tournament staged at Binche in 1549, with special reference to the imperial myth in relation to its use of chivalry.

CALVETE DE ESTRELLA, *Le Très-Heureux Voyage fait ... par Don Philippe fils du grand Empereur Charles-Quint*, Société des Bibliophiles de Belgique, 16 (Brussels 1884).
Account of the future Philip II's tour of Italy, Germany and the Low Countries in 1548–9, with full descriptions of the fêtes staged en route.

JEAN JACQUOT, 'Panorame des Fêtes et Cérémonies du Regne', in *Les Fêtes de la Renaissance*, ed. J. Jacquot, II, CNRS (1960), *Fêtes et Cérémonies au Temps de Charles Quint*, pp. 413–86.
The only survey of the festivals for the whole reign of Charles V.

MARCEL LAGEIRSE, 'La Joyeuse Entrée du Prince Philippe à Gand en 1549', in *Les Fêtes de la Renaissance*, ed. J. Jacquot, II, CNRS (1960), *Fêtes et Cérémonies au Temps de Charles Quint*, pp. 297–306.
Publishes the engravings of Philip II's entry in 1549 and discusses their importance as examples of *à l'antique* architecture.

ALBERT VAN DE PUT, 'Two Drawings of the Fêtes at Binche for Charles V and Philip II, 1549', *Journal of the Warburg and Courtauld Institutes* (1939–40), pp. 49–57.
Publishes the only two illustrations of the Binche fêtes.

SANTIAGO SEBASTIAN, 'La exaltación de Carlos V en la arquitectura mallorquina del siglo XVI', *Mayurqa, Miscelánea de Estudios Humanisticos*, V (1971), pp. 99–113.
Discussion of Charles V's entry into Mallorca, reproducing the extremely rare woodcuts of the pageants.

VICOMTE TERLINDEN, 'La Politique Italienne de Charles Quint et le "Triomphe" de Bologne', in *Les Fêtes de la Renaissance*, ed. J. Jacquot, II, CNRS (Paris 1960), *Fêtes et Cérémonies au Temps de Charles Quint*, pp. 29–43.
Political background to the imperial coronation of 1530.

LATE VALOIS COURT FESTIVALS

ROY STRONG, 'Festivals for the Garter Embassy at the Court of Henry III', *Journal of Warburg and Courtauld Institutes*, XXII (1959), pp. 60–70.
Account of Henry III's reception of the Order of the Garter in 1585 with an English description of a ballet given to mark the occasion. An interesting example of the use of chivalry as a means of bridging the gap between Catholic and Protestant.

CORRADO VIVANTI, 'Henry IV, The Gallic Hercules', *Journal of the Warburg and Courtauld Institutes*, XXX, 1967, pp. 176–97.
Traces the role of Henry IV as the Messianic ruler with an imperial destiny, including discussions of State entries.

FRANCES A. YATES, 'Dramatic Religious Processions in Paris in the late Sixteenth Century', *Annales Musicologues*, II (1954), pp. 215–62.
Description of street processions in Paris organized by Henry III and later by the Holy League and their historical connotation.

FRANCES A. YATES, 'Poèsie et Musique dans les "Magnificences" au Mariage du Duc de Joyeuse, Paris 1581', in *Musique et Poèsie au XVIe Siècle*, CNRS (Paris 1954), pp. 241–63.
Important article reconstituting the fêtes for the marriage of Henry III's favourite, Joyeuse.

FRANCES A. YATES, 'Poètes et Artistes dans les Entrées de Charles IX et de sa Reine à Paris en 1571', in *Les Fêtes de la Renaissance*, ed. J. Jacquot, CNRS (Paris 1956), pp. 61–91.
Analysis of the mythology of the entries of Charles IX and his Queen into Paris in 1571 and the part played by humanists of the Academy in devising the programme.

FRANCES A. YATES, *The French Academies of the Sixteenth Century* (London 1947).
Chapter IX is fundamental for an understanding of late Valois festivals and, in particular, contains the fundamental exegesis of the *Balet Comique de la Reyne* of 1581.

FRANCES A. YATES, *The Valois Tapestries* (London 1959).
The most comprehensive discussion of late Valois court fêtes, centring on a discussion of the Valois Tapestries in the Uffizi.

MEDICI COURT FESTIVALS

GIROLAMO BARGAGLI, *La Pellegrina*, ed. Florindo Correta, Biblioteca dell'Archivum Romanicum, serie I, III (1971).
Edition of the play used for the 1589 intermezzi.

GIOVANNA MARIA BERTELÀ and ANNAMARIA PETRIOLI TOFANI, *Feste e Apparati Medicei da Cosimo I a Cosimo II*, Mostra di Disegni e Incisioni, Gabinetto di Disegni e Stampe degli Uffizi, XXXI (1969).
Fundamental publication for the study of Medici fêtes, including reproductions of designs for scenery and costumes and a valuable bibliography.

E. BORSOOK, 'Art and Politics at the Medici Court. I: The Funeral of Cosimo I de'Medici', *Mitteilungen des Kunsthistorischen Institutes in Florenz*, XII (1965), pp. 31–54.
The first of a series of articles by Eve Borsook which, for the first time, present accurately documented and substantially analysed accounts of Medici festivals.

E. BORSOOK, 'Drawings for the Funeral of Cosimo I de'Medici', *Mitteilungen des Kunsthistorischen Institutes in Florenz*, XII (1966), pp. 366–71.

E. BORSOOK, 'Art and Politics at the Medici Court. II: The Baptism of Filippo de'Medici in 1577', *Mitteilungen des Kunsthistorischen Institutes in Florenz*, XIII (1967), pp. 95–114.

E. BORSOOK, 'Art and Politics at the Medici Court. III: Funeral Décor for Philip II of Spain', *Mitteilungen des Kunsthistorischen Institutes in Florenz*, XV (1969), pp. 91–114.

E. BORSOOK, 'Art and Politics at the Medici Court. IV: Funeral Décor for Henry IV of France', *Mitteilungen des Kunsthistorischen Institutes in Florenz*, XV (1969), pp. 201–43.

ANDREW C. MINOR and BONNER MITCHELL (eds), *A Renaissance Entertainment: Festivities for the Marriage of Cosimo I, Duke of Florence, in 1539* (Missouri 1968).
Account of the festivities marking Cosimo I's marriage to Eleanor of Toledo in 1539.

A. M. NAGLER, *Theatre Festivals of Medici, 1539–1637* (New Haven 1964).
Useful narrative of Medici fêtes with the best collection of plates. Virtually no attempt is made to analyse their content or meaning and the omission of State entries into Florence is a mistake.

A. M. PETRIOLI, *Mostra di disegni vasariani. Carri trionfali e costumi per la Genealogia degli Dei (1565)*, Gabinetto di Disegni e Stampe degli Uffizi (1966).
Exhibition of designs for the famous masquerade of 1566 to celebrate the marriage of Francesco de'Medici and Joanna of Austria.

LEO SCHRADE, 'Les Fêtes du Mariage de Francesco de' Medici et de Bianca Cappello', in *Les Fêtes de la Renaissance*, ed. J. Jacquot, CNRS (Paris 1956), pp. 107–30.
Important analysis of the *Sbarra* of 1579, its mythology and music.

ANGELO SOLERTI, *Musica, Ballo e Drammatica alla Corte Medicea dal 1600 al 1637* (Florence 1905).
Dated guide to Medici court festivals.

D. P. WALKER (ed.), *Les Fêtes du Mariage de Ferdinand de Médicis et de Christine de*

Lorraine, Florence 1589, I, Musique des Intermèdes de 'La Pellegrina', CNRS (Paris 1963).
The most important study of the intermezzi of 1589 with an edition of the music. A second volume is promised on the State entry and other fêtes.

ABY WARBURG, 'I Costumi Teatrali per gli Intermezzi del 1589', in *Gesammelte Schriften* I (Leipzig 1932).

TUDOR AND EARLY STUART FESTIVALS

SYDNEY ANGLO, 'La Salle de Banquet et le Théâtre construits à Greenwich pour les Fêtes Franco-Anglaises de 1527', in *Le Lieu Théâtral à la Renaissance*, ed. J. Jacquot, CNRS (Paris 1964), pp. 273–88.
Festivals for the reception of a French embassy and an account of the banqueting hall especially erected for the occasion with decorations by Holbein.

SYDNEY ANGLO, *Spectacle, Pageantry and Early Tudor Policy* (London 1969).
The fundamental survey of all fêtes from the accession of Henry VII up to and including the pageants for the coronation of Elizabeth I. Extremely valuable for its documentation.

SYDNEY ANGLO, 'The Court Festivals of Henry VII; A Study based upon the Account Books of John Heron, Treasurer of the Chamber', *Bulletin of the John Rylands Library*, 43, 1 (1960), pp. 12–45.

SYDNEY ANGLO, 'The Foundation of the Tudor Dynasty: the Coronation and Marriage of Henry VII', *The Guildhall Miscellany*, II, xi (1960), pp. 3–31.

SYDNEY ANGLO, *The Great Tournament Roll of Westminster* (Oxford 1968).
Facsimile reproduction of an illuminated roll recording the tournament given by Henry VIII in 1511 to celebrate the birth of a Prince of Wales. The introduction contains the best account of the early Tudor chivalry.

DAVID M. BERGERON, *English Civic Pageantry, 1558–1642* (London 1971).
Useful survey of royal entries with a bibliography, but disappointing in its failure to analyse the content of the fêtes.

JOYCELYNE C. RUSSELL, *The Field of Cloth of Gold, Men and Manners in 1520* (London 1969).
The best account of the Field of Cloth of Gold.

ROY STRONG, 'The Popular Celebration of the Accession Day of Queen Elizabeth I', *Journal of the Warburg and Courtauld Institutes*, XXI (1958), pp. 86–103.
An instance of the development of secular celebrations to replace pre-Reformation religious festivals.

FRANCES A. YATES, 'Elizabethan Chivalry: the Romance of the Accession Day Tilts', *Journal of the Warburg and Courtauld Institutes*, XX (1957), pp. 4–25.
Account of the deliberate use of chivalry in relation to the glorification of the Crown in Elizabethan England.

THE STUART COURT MASQUES
The literature on these is now very considerable. Included here are only the most significant studies.

W. TODD FURNISS, 'Ben Jonson's Masques', in *Yale Studies in English*, 138 (Yale 1958).
Interesting discussion of Jonson's use of Golden Age and pastoral motifs in relation to the Stuart monarchy.

D. J. GORDON, 'The Imagery of Ben Jonson's *The Masque of Blacknesse* and the *Masque of Beautie*', *Journal of the Warburg and Courtauld Institutes*, VI (1943), pp. 101–21.
The fundamental article on the meaning of Jonson's masques and a model of analytical method in relation to studying the masques in depth.

D. J. GORDON, '*Hymenaei*: Ben Jonson's Masque of Union', *Journal of the Warburg and Courtauld Institutes*, VIII (1945), pp. 107–45.
Following the method used in his previous article on the *Masque of Blacknesse* and the *Masque of Beautie*, a brilliant analysis of the meaning of a Jonson masque.

D. J. GORDON, 'Le "Masque Mémorable" de Chapman', in *Les Fêtes de la Renaissance*, ed. J. Jacquot, CNRS (Paris 1956), pp. 305–17.
Important analysis of Chapman's masque for the marriage of the Princess Elizabeth to the Elector Palatine in 1613, with deliberate use of Orphic chanting and Neo-Platonic magic.

D. J. GORDON, 'Poet and Architect: the Intellectual Setting of the Quarrel between Ben Jonson and Inigo Jones', *Journal of the Warburg and Courtauld Institutes*, XII (1949), pp. 152–78.
A penetrating glimpse into the thought premises that governed the contributions made to a Renaissance spectacle by the poet and the architect.

JEAN JACQUOT, 'La Reine Henriette Marie et l'influence française dans les spectacles à la cour de Charles Ier', *9e Cahier de l'association international des études françaises* (Paris 1957).
French influences on the Caroline masques.

M.-T. JONES-DAVIES, *Inigo Jones, Ben Jonson et le Masque* (Paris 1967).
Recent account which adds little to our knowledge of the masque.

JOHN C. MEAGHER, 'The Dance and the Masques of Ben Jonson', *Journal of the Warburg and Courtauld Institutes*, XXV (1962), pp. 258–00.
Analysis of the use and meaning of the dance in Jonson's masques and, by implication, of its meaning generally in Renaissance festivals.

JOHN C. MEAGHER, *Methods and Meaning in Ben Jonson's Masques* (Notre Dame 1966).

ALLARDYCE NICOLL, *Stuart Masques and the Renaissance Stage* (Edinburgh 1937).
Pioneer work on the relationship of Inigo Jones's work on the masque to Italian prototypes. This book is now superseded by Orgel and Strong listed below.

STEPHEN ORGEL, *The Jonsonian Masque* (Cambridge, Mass. 1965).
The most important recent book on the masque from the literary aspect.

STEPHEN ORGEL, 'The Poetics of Spectacle', *New Literary History*, II, 3 (spring 1971), pp. 367–89.

STEPHEN ORGEL, 'To Make Boards to Speak: Inigo Jones's Stage and the Jonsonian Masque', *Renaissance Drama*, new series I (1968), pp. 121–52.

STEPHEN ORGEL and ROY STRONG, *Inigo Jones. The Theatre of the Stuart Court* (London 1973).
Contains the complete texts, historical documentation, designs and sources of all masques and entertainments associated with Inigo Jones. This book also includes the only detailed discussion of the Caroline masques.

PAUL REHYER, *Les Masques Anglais* (Paris 1909).
Although dated this book is still valuable, particularly for its mass of historical data.

ENID WELSFORD, *The Court Masque* (Cambridge 1927).
A pioneer work in its day, this book has now been entirely superseded by the work of Gordon and Orgel.

FESTIVALS AT MINOR COURTS
Bavaria

GÜNTER SCHÖNE, 'Les Fêtes de la Renaissance à la cour de Bavière', in *Le Lieu Théâtral à la Renaissance*, ed. J. Jacquot, CNRS (Paris 1964), pp. 171–82.
Festivals of the reign of Duke Albert V (1550–79) and in particular those to celebrate the marriage of his son to Renée of Lorraine in 1568.

Lorraine

F. G. PARISET, 'Le Mariage d'Henri de Lorraine et de Marguerite Gonazague-Mantoue (1606)', in *Les Fêtes de la Renaissance*, ed. J. Jacquot, CNRS (Paris 1956), pp. 153–86.

Extremely important article on these fêtes with valuable background information on the civilization of the court of Lorraine at the time when Jacques Bellange was in ducal service.

The Netherlands

J. A. VAN DORSTEN and ROY STRONG, *Leicester's Triumph* (Leiden 1964).
Account of the fêtes held in 1585–6 to welcome the Earl of Leicester as Governor-General of the Low Countries, and of their political implications.

Savoy

MERCEDES VIALE FERRERO, *Feste delle Madame Reali di Savoia* (Turin 1965).
Excellent introduction to Savoy court fêtes in the first half of the seventeenth century, profusely illustrated.

MARGARET MCGOWAN, 'Les fêtes de Cour en Savoie. L'Oeuvre de Philippe d'Aglié', *Revue d'Histoire du Théâtre*, III (1970), pp. 183–242.
Important analysis of Aglié's work at the Savoy court.

Italy

P. DE NOLHAC and A. SOLERTI, *Il Viaggio in Italia di Enrico III* (Turin 1890).
Account of festivals for Henry III en route from Poland to France, 1574.

Genealogical Trees

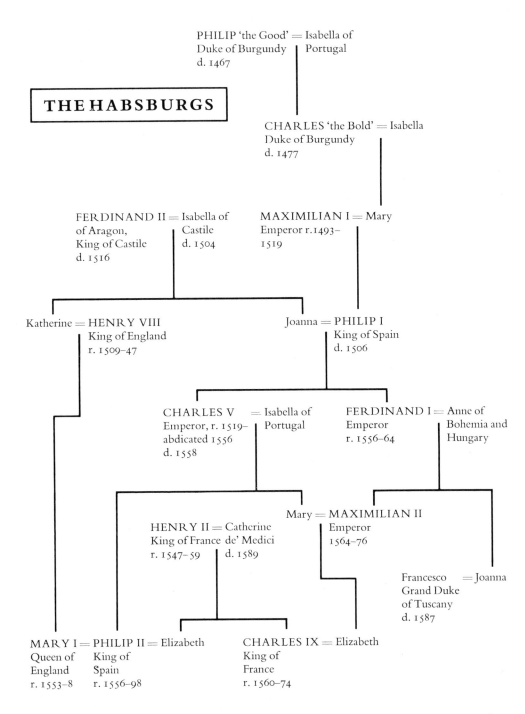

THE HABSBURGS

PHILIP 'the Good' = Isabella of
Duke of Burgundy | Portugal
d. 1467

CHARLES 'the Bold' = Isabella
Duke of Burgundy
d. 1477

FERDINAND II = Isabella of   MAXIMILIAN I = Mary
of Aragon,   Castile   Emperor r.1493–
King of Castile d. 1504   1519
d. 1516

Katherine = HENRY VIII   Joanna = PHILIP I
            King of England   King of Spain
            r. 1509–47   d. 1506

CHARLES V = Isabella of   FERDINAND I = Anne of
Emperor, r. 1519– Portugal   Emperor   Bohemia and
abdicated 1556   r. 1556–64   Hungary
d. 1558

HENRY II = Catherine   Mary = MAXIMILIAN II
King of France de' Medici   Emperor
r. 1547–59   d. 1589   1564–76

                          Francesco   = Joanna
                          Grand Duke
                          of Tuscany
                          d. 1587

MARY I = PHILIP II = Elizabeth   CHARLES IX = Elizabeth
Queen of King of   King of
England   Spain   France
r. 1553–8 r. 1556–98   r. 1560–74

VALOIS AND BOURBON

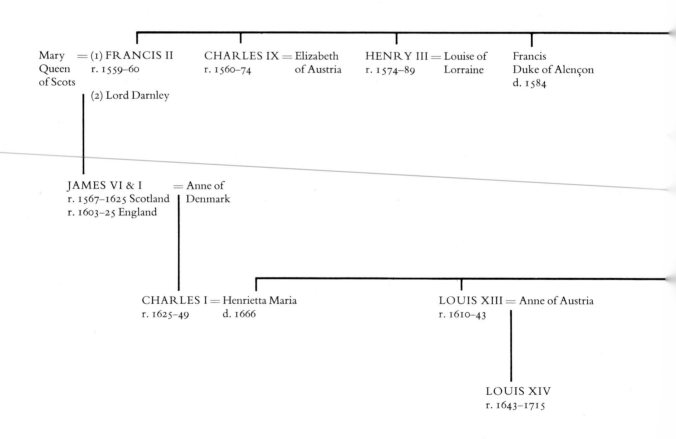

Mary Queen of Scots = (1) FRANCIS II r. 1559–60

CHARLES IX r. 1560–74 = Elizabeth of Austria

HENRY III r. 1574–89 = Louise of Lorraine

Francis Duke of Alençon d. 1584

(2) Lord Darnley

JAMES VI & I r. 1567–1625 Scotland r. 1603–25 England = Anne of Denmark

CHARLES I r. 1625–49 = Henrietta Maria d. 1666

LOUIS XIII r. 1610–43 = Anne of Austria

LOUIS XIV r. 1643–1715

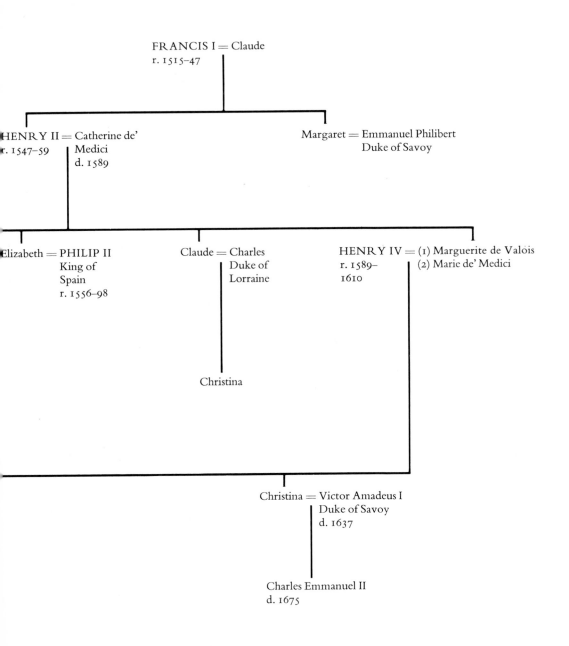

FRANCIS I = Claude
r. 1515–47

HENRY II = Catherine de'
r. 1547–59 | Medici
d. 1589

Margaret = Emmanuel Philibert
Duke of Savoy

Elizabeth = PHILIP II
King of
Spain
r. 1556–98

Claude = Charles
Duke of
Lorraine

HENRY IV = (1) Marguerite de Valois
r. 1589–
1610 | (2) Marie de' Medici

Christina

Christina = Victor Amadeus I
Duke of Savoy
d. 1637

Charles Emmanuel II
d. 1675

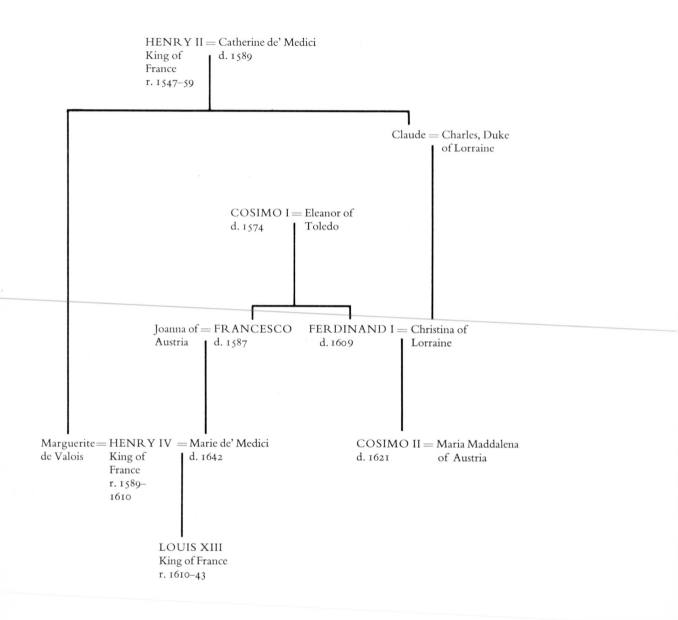

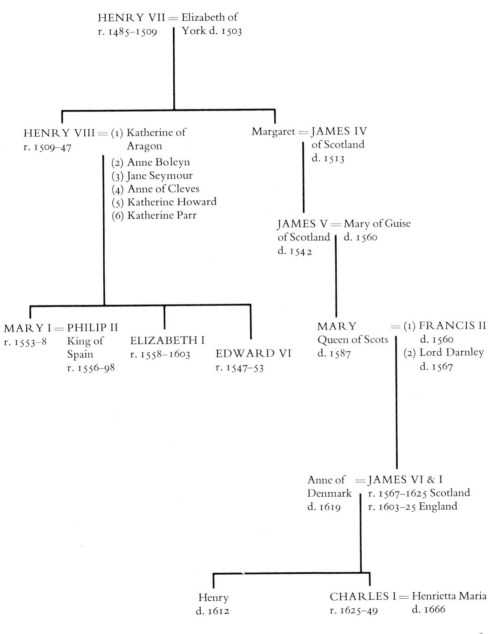

THE TUDORS AND STUARTS

HENRY VII = Elizabeth of
r. 1485–1509   York d. 1503

HENRY VIII = (1) Katherine of
r. 1509–47   Aragon
           (2) Anne Boleyn
           (3) Jane Seymour
           (4) Anne of Cleves
           (5) Katherine Howard
           (6) Katherine Parr

Margaret = JAMES IV
         of Scotland
         d. 1513

JAMES V = Mary of Guise
of Scotland   d. 1560
d. 1542

MARY I = PHILIP II
r. 1553–8   King of
        Spain
        r. 1556–98

ELIZABETH I
r. 1558–1603

EDWARD VI
r. 1547–53

MARY = (1) FRANCIS II
Queen of Scots   d. 1560
d. 1587   (2) Lord Darnley
            d. 1567

Anne of = JAMES VI & I
Denmark   r. 1567–1625 Scotland
d. 1619   r. 1603–25 England

Henry
d. 1612

CHARLES I = Henrietta Maria
r. 1625–49   d. 1666

267

Habsburg

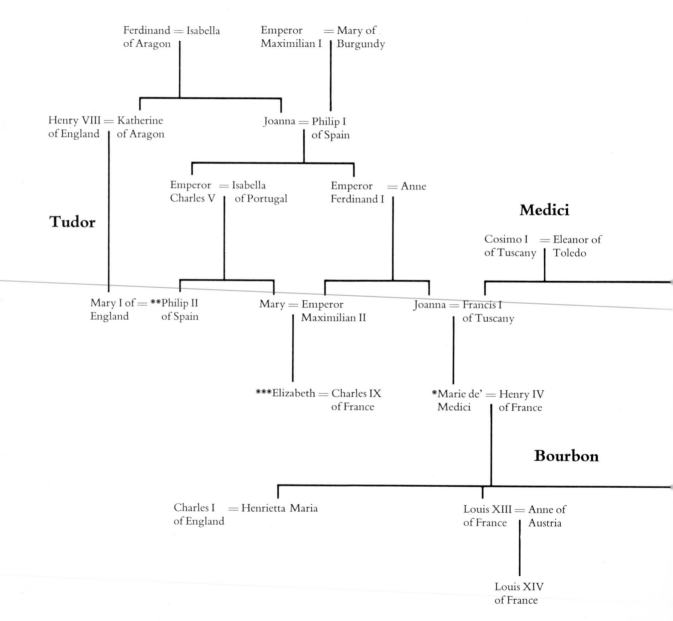

Ferdinand = Isabella
of Aragon

Emperor = Mary of
Maximilian I | Burgundy

Henry VIII = Katherine
of England | of Aragon

Joanna = Philip I
of Spain

Emperor = Isabella
Charles V | of Portugal

Emperor = Anne
Ferdinand I

Medici

Cosimo I = Eleanor of
of Tuscany | Toledo

Tudor

Mary I of = **Philip II
England | of Spain

Mary = Emperor
Maximilian II

Joanna = Francis I
of Tuscany

***Elizabeth = Charles IX
of France

*Marie de' = Henry IV
Medici | of France

Bourbon

Charles I = Henrietta Maria
of England

Louis XIII = Anne of
of France | Austria

Louis XIV
of France

CONNECTIONS BETWEEN THE RULING HOUSES OF EUROPE

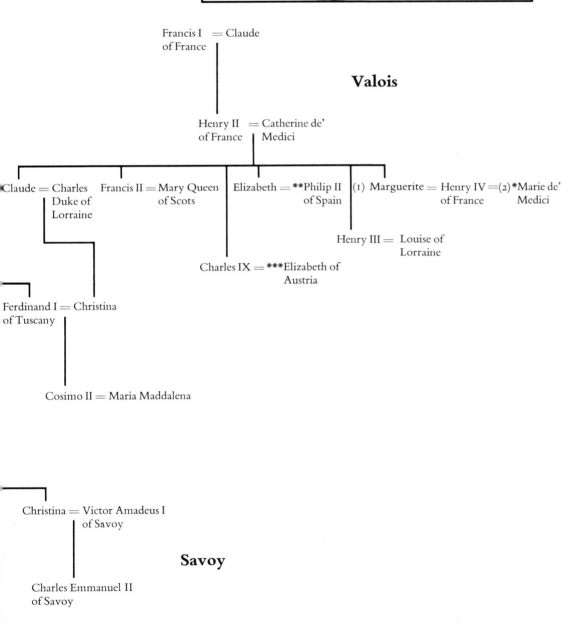

Francis I = Claude
of France

Valois

Henry II = Catherine de'
of France Medici

Claude = Charles   Francis II = Mary Queen   Elizabeth = **Philip II   (1) Marguerite = Henry IV =(2)*Marie de'
Duke of   of Scots   of Spain   of France   Medici
Lorraine

Henry III = Louise of
Lorraine

Charles IX = ***Elizabeth of
Austria

Ferdinand I = Christina
of Tuscany

Cosimo II = Maria Maddalena

Christina = Victor Amadeus I
of Savoy

Savoy

Charles Emmanuel II
of Savoy

List of Colour Plates and Figures

COLOUR PLATES

I *Carrousel for the marriage of Duchess Christina's daughter, Adelaide, to Ferdinand of Bavaria, 1650.* Detail of drawing from *Gli Hercoli domatori de' Mostri et Amore domatori degli Hercoli, Festa a Cavallo per la Reali Nozze dell S.P. Adelaide de Savoia et del S.P. Ferdinando Maria ...* Biblioteca Nazionale Universitaria, Turin, B.R.N. 13 344 (Photo: Chomon-Perino)

II *Allegorical Banquet given at Rivoli for the Birthday of Duchess Christina of Savoy, 1645.* Drawing from *Dono del Re dell'Alpi a Madama Reale festa per il giorno natale li 10 feb.*, Biblioteca Nazionale Universitaria, Turin, B.R. Q V 60 (Photo: Chomon-Perino)

III Rubens, *Sketch of the Arch of the Mint for the Entry of the Cardinal Archduke Ferdinand, 1635.* Painting, Koninlijk Museum, Antwerp (Photo: De Schutter)

IV *Carrousel to celebrate the Duke of Savoy's Birthday, 1645.* Drawing from *L'Oriente guerriera et festiggiante, Carozello, festa a cavallo fatta al Valentino per il giorno natale de S.A.S. li 10 giugno.* Biblioteca Nazionale Universitaria, Turin, B.Naz. Q V 52 (Photo: Chomon-Perino)

V *Francis I's Entry into Lyon, 1515.* Illuminations. The Ducal Library, Wolfenbüttel, Cod. Guelf. 86.4 (Photos: Ducal Library)

VI *Henry II's Entry into Rouen, 1550.* Illumination in the *Entrée de Henri II à Rouen le Ier Octobre 1550*, Rouen, Bibliothèque Municipale (Photo: Ellebe)

VII *Tournament ceremonial* from Réné of Anjou's *Traité de la forme et devis d'un tournois.* Illuminations from Paris, Bibliothèque Nationale MS. Fr. 2695v (Photos: Bibl. Nat.)

VIII *The Valois Tapestries. Court ball following the 'Ballet of the Provinces of France', 1573.* Detail. Uffizi Gallery, Florence (Photo: Scala)

IX *The Valois Tapestries. Unidentified Festival. Assault upon an Elephant.* Detail. Uffizi Gallery, Florence (Photo: Scala)

X *The Valois Tapestries. Tourney of the Knights of Great Britain and Ireland, Bayonne, 1565.* Detail. Uffizi Gallery, Florence (Photo: Scala)

XI Bernardo Buontalenti, *Design for Necessity and the Fates for the first intermezzo, 1589.* Drawing. Biblioteca Nazionale Centrale, Florence (Photo: Library)

270

Beaujoyeulx, *Le Balet Comique de la Reyne, 1581* (Photos: Warburg Institute)

Inigo Jones, *Design for a tournament helmet, c. 1610*

Index

Mythological, biblical and other characters
who appear in the festivals are printed in italic.